The Land Before Avocado

'This is vintage Glover – warm, wise and very, very funny.
Brimming with excruciating insights into life in the late sixties
and early seventies, *The Land Before Avocado* explains why this
was the cultural revolution we had to have' – Hugh Mackay

'Hilarious and horrifying, this is the ultimate intergenerational
conversation starter' – Annabel Crabb

Richard Glover's just-published *The Land Before
Avocado* is a wonderful and witty journey back in time to
life in the early 1970s'
– Richard Wakelin, *Australian Financial Review*

Flesh Wounds

'A funny, moving, very entertaining memoir'
– Bill Bryson, *New York Times*

'Not since Unreliable Memoirs by Clive James has there been a
funnier, more poignant portrait of an Australian childhood'
– *The Australian Financial Review*

Richard Glover has written a number of bestselling books, including *The Land Before Avocado*, *Flesh Wounds* and *The Mud House*. He writes regularly for the *Sydney Morning Herald* and *The Washington Post*, as well as presenting the comedy program *Thank God It's Friday* on ABC Local Radio. To find out more, visit www.richardglover.com.au

Love, Clancy

A Dog's Letters Home

Richard Glover

ABC
BOOKS

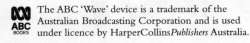 The ABC 'Wave' device is a trademark of the
Australian Broadcasting Corporation and is used
under licence by HarperCollins*Publishers* Australia.

HarperCollins*Publishers*
Australia • Brazil • Canada • France • Germany • Holland • Hungary
India • Italy • Japan • Mexico • New Zealand • Poland • Spain • Sweden
Switzerland • United Kingdom • United States of America

First published in Australia in 2020
by HarperCollins*Publishers* Australia Pty Limited
Level 13, 201 Elizabeth Street, Sydney NSW 2000
ABN 36 009 913 517
harpercollins.com.au

ISBN 978 0 7333 4106 9 (paperback)
ISBN 978 1 4607 1280 1 (ebook)

Cover design by Amy Daoud, HarperCollins Design Studio
Cover photography: Jon Lewis (front); Debra Oswald (back)
Illustrations by Cathy Wilcox
Author photo by Marco del Grande
Typeset in Adobe Caslon Pro by Kirby Jones
Printed and bound in Australia by McPherson's Printing Group
The papers used by HarperCollins in the manufacture of this book are a natural, recyclable product
made from wood grown in sustainable plantation forests. The fibre source and manufacturing pro-
cesses meet recognised international environmental standards, and carry certification.

To Pepper

Introduction

Have you had the experience of calling out to your new dog, but using the name of your old dog by mistake? It happens to me all the time. It's like a scene out of *Rebecca*, Daphne du Maurier's novel about a household haunted by its previous queen.

'Come here, Darcy, I mean Clancy. Oh, damn, sorry.'

Of course, I love my new dog – fit as a fiddle, eyes bright and ears keen. But there is something about an old dog: the way in which the body may be weak but the spirit is still so eager.

My old dog ended up deaf, so he couldn't hear me coming in the front door. I'd clatter up the hallway shouting his name as I'd done for years, and then into the kitchen where he'd be slumbering oblivious on a rug. Then, as I leant over to pat him, Darcy would suddenly see me. His head would tilt quizzically, the eyes suddenly gleaming like those of a puppy, as if to say: 'What's next, boss? Where are we off to now?'

These maudlin thoughts were intensified thanks to the book *An Odyssey* by the American writer Daniel Mendelsohn. It's a tender account of teaching Homer's *Odyssey* to an undergraduate class whose ranks have been swelled by Mendelsohn's irascible 81-year-old father. Amid the family drama, the book offers a retelling of Homer's poem, including the emotional climax: the moment when Odysseus finally returns to Ithaca after two decades of travails.

It's a scene involving an old, loyal dog.

The Homeric epics date from about 800 BC. That's a long time ago. The poems provide evidence for the early importance of dogs – not just for their hunting ability or their role guarding the camp, but for their emotional succour. In *The Odyssey*, the hero returns home wearing a disguise so that he might assess the loyalty of his household. As Odysseus – dressed as an old beggar – walks up to the gates of his palace, a mangy dog is lying on a dung heap outside the palace walls. It is the loyal dog Argos, trained as a puppy by Odysseus, and then abandoned – 'an object of revulsion, his master long since gone'.

The humans are fooled by the disguise, but not so the dog. In Mendelsohn's translation:

When he sensed that Odysseus was close by
He wagged his tail and lay his ears down flat,
But no longer has the strength to come to his master.

Heartbreakingly, in order to protect his disguise, Odysseus cannot acknowledge the dog's existence. He just walks past – his inner

2

torment expressed through a single tear, which rolls down his cheek.

Next, says Homer:

Death's darkness then took hold of Argos, who
had seen Odysseus again, after twenty years.

Argos can die because he knows his master is now safely home. That, for him, is even more important than his master's touch.

It's hard not to cry at the scene, dog lover or not. I'm sobbing a little myself as I type out Homer's words for you, sentimental fool that I am. My young dog, Clancy, half-asleep on my bed, jumps up in order to investigate these strange choking noises coming from my throat. He stands next to my office chair and rests his chin on my lap, his tail wagging, demanding I pat him, glancing up at me to check I'm okay. Like all dogs, he has this curious ability to demand love as a means of supplying it.

Clancy's concern reminds me of other dogs in world literature. For instance: Sashenka, the dog in Tolstoy's *War and Peace*. At the end of the BBC's adaptation of the book, Pierre Bezukhov is struggling to find meaning in life. He remembers the peasant who owned Sashenka and how that man talked about his little dog's spirit.

'She knows how to ask for love,' Pierre remembers the peasant saying, 'and she knows to give it. What else can you ask?'

Thinking of this scene tips me into further weird choking noises, which further panic Clancy, leading to more nuzzling, more patting and more anxious upwards glances.

Argos. Sashenka. Darcy. Clancy.

Maybe all this emotion is not about old dogs and young dogs; not even about my old dog Darcy and my new dog Clancy. It's just about dogs.

When Darcy died, it seemed impossible that a new dog could ever enter our lives. After we lost him, at the age of fifteen, misery seemed to fill every part of the house. There was not a corner of the place that didn't hold a memory. In the bedroom, it was the recollection of me reading the newspaper at the start of every day, holding the *Sydney Morning Herald* in one hand as I stroked his head with the other, his outrage palpable when I tried to move my hand to turn the page.

I'd try to explain – 'I've finished the Julia Baird column. I need to move on' – but Darcy would just push his muzzle more firmly towards me, as if to say, 'I think you'll find she's worth reading twice.'

Or in the kitchen, the way he'd suddenly appear, head cocked to one side, eyes quizzical, whenever the fridge door was opened.

'While you're there, I don't suppose you'd mind fetching a small slice of cheese?'

Or in the back room, where Darcy could find some early-morning sun to bask in, his black fur hot to the touch, as if he were a battery, recharging himself.

They say, in the moments before death your life is replayed at high speed. I don't know if that's true, but as I walked home from the vet, an empty dog collar in my hand, my partner sobbing beside me, scenes from Darcy's life filled my head.

We'd picked him up from a farm near Orange, almost 15 years before, a tiny kelpie puppy. He'd sat in the back seat of the car, nestled between our two young children, his head tucked down into his own body, too nervous to look around. He grew bigger, the boys grew bigger. I wonder now whether I was weeping for him or for a time of life that had passed.

Like all dogs, Darcy had a personality of his own. Thoughtful rather than rambunctious; listening hard to understand what people were saying; anxious when it came to his personal nemesis the Wheelie Bin; joyful when he was around wind or water.

He was always eager to be trained. When we first took him walking, he'd overhear us talking about whether it was time to turn for home. Soon he'd created his own dog-training command, looking up with a searching gaze for any mention of the word 'turn'. Over the next few weeks, he put in effort to train his humans. In the end, we understood what he was after: at the furthest part of our usual walk, we were to stop, allow him to adopt a racing position, then deliver the brisk order – 'turn' – at which point he would pivot, sprint for 200 metres back the way we came, pause, then swivel to face us.

If dogs could take a bow, he would have done so. It's a miracle he didn't offer us a liver treat once we'd finally managed to grasp his instructions.

Every dog has lessons to teach. They are experts, as I mentioned, in demanding love. Humans often doubt whether they are worthy of love, but dogs have no such uncertainty. 'Look at me, just look at me,' Darcy would say and, as my eyes met his, it was impossible not to submit to his demand for a compliment.

'What a good dog. What a handsome dog. You are the best dog that ever was.'

Then Darcy would return the favour, looking back as if to say: 'What's next, boss? You, after all, are my favourite human and I would follow you anywhere, through hot deserts or raging streams or high mountains.'

This giving and receiving of love seems so right, so nourishing, one sometimes wonders whether it might have useful application outside the world of dogs. It's a utopian idea, I know, but perhaps worth a try.

The hallway in our house is lined with family pictures, mostly from the time when the children were small. In many of them, Darcy is featured, pictured with our boys, often on summer holidays. He looks towards the camera and so do my two young sons. He is black and tan. They are blond and sun-reddened.

Every corner of the house is full of memories, but the hallway is the worst. On that first night, I returned from work in the early evening. It was about ten hours since that final visit to the vet. I came up the front steps and put the key in the lock. The children had grown up and moved out, so there was no rumble of noise from them. And, of course, there was no clatter of paws, rushing towards me, as if to say, 'Oh, boss, it's been so long. Oh, boss, where have you been?'

Worse things have happened to you and worse things have happened to me, but there's nothing like the death of a good dog to bring tears that are so hot and unrestrained.

Perhaps it's because a dog, a really good dog, is just love, pure love.

After Darcy died, we rang the people from whom we'd acquired him all those years ago. We thought they'd like to know. Then, towards the end of the phone call, there was a moment's silence, and then an offer.

'You know, we've just had a new litter of puppies, and one of them isn't spoken for ...'

And so a month later, I'm in the backyard, playing with my new puppy. He is a tiny kelpie, and he sits on the back step watching everything I do with an intense curiosity. He is ten weeks old. He is as adorable as your imagination might care to make him.

We purchased an up-to-date training manual, so that he might end up as spectacular a dog as Darcy. The book required the humans to do some acting. If the dog is at the back step, whining to be allowed inside, you cannot reward the behaviour by opening the door. This, the manual says, is very bad practice. Instead, you should head out into the yard, as if on a task of your own invention – 'I wonder if my lemons are ripe?' – then express surprise when you see the puppy waiting by the door. At which point you may let them in – leaving the dog to believe itself lucky rather than victorious.

The book also says you shouldn't shout at them if they urinate on the floor. Better to express disappointment as you carry them outside. 'Oh, that's a shame. Oh, what a setback. I feel very sad.'

And – the book insists – it's wrong to be angry if they nip you during play. Better to express pain: 'Oh, that hurt. You hurt me so badly then. It really is quite sore.'

Plus, a final overarching instruction: if the puppy won't do as you request, you should act 'astonished'. 'What? You won't sit down? Wow, I've never heard of a puppy that refused to carry out such a simple request. This behaviour of yours really does leave me feeling quite discombobulated.'

Back in the yard, in the deepening dusk, I finish up at the lemon tree and turn back towards the door, pausing as I pretend to spot the little puppy, who is sitting patiently, waiting and watching.

'Oh, there you are,' I say with a gush of feigned surprise. 'I was just outside checking my lemons, which are not ready for picking, but since we're here, would you like to come in?'

He tilts his head to one side in the quizzical way of the kelpie. Already he is finding my performance a little overblown. In that puzzled head tilt there is a complete theatrical review: 'The acting is terrible, the lines overwritten and the plot impossible to believe. The lemons, for a start, are entirely green, so by what plausible logic could they be considered ready for picking?'

He then leans his tiny head the opposite way as if to give his final judgement: 'One star.'

It was only later, when he began writing his letters home, that I fully understood the sort of dog I'd chanced upon. He was one clever animal, and that cleverness was about to be utilised in describing the world in which he had found himself.

After losing our precious Darcy, it turned out that our grief had only one answer, and his name was Clancy.

These are his letters home.

Age: **Three months**

C/- The New Kennel

Chateau Chaos

28 November

Dear Mum and Dad,

It's Clancy here, your puppy, writing from my new home in the city. The people I've moved in with seem friendly but a little strange. They're particularly weird whenever I urinate. Either they run around grabbing rolls of paper towel, in a scene of some hysteria, saying, 'Oh no! Oh no!' or they stand smiling and saying, 'Good dog, good dog.'

The first version happens inside, after I've urinated on the kitchen floor; the other outside, after I've urinated on the grass. I'm not sure what they are trying to convey. The only certain thing is that the 'Oh no! Oh no!' version is much more fun for me to watch, so it's the reaction I go out of my way to generate.

The two of them seem easy-going. They attempted to ban me from the bed, which gave me the incentive to develop my jumping skills. I now take a run-up along the hall, make a sharp right-turn into the bedroom doorway … and then leap. I'm not so much a jumping dog at this point, more a low-flying buzz bomb. If I time it right, I can maintain cruising altitude for the full length of the bed before landing directly on the man's head. He says, 'It's like being in London during the Blitz,' a reference which leaves me puzzled, as he appears to be of insufficient age to have experienced that particular horror. (They have a big-screen TV, and I've been watching quite a few history documentaries when they are out, and World War II is featured quite regularly.)

In terms of the man, the weirdest thing is that he has a bicycle in the shed, but it has no wheels. He goes out there and pedals away, sweating and groaning and puffing, but the bike never moves. Whenever he gets on it – which, admittedly, is not that often – I run around in circles, trying to tell him that he's bought a bike that doesn't work. Alas, he just gets annoyed, which I suppose is reasonable given the way he's been so badly ripped off.

On the positive side, the couple has kindly filled the house full of toys perfect for a new puppy. The lady, for instance, has an attractive wicker wastepaper basket beneath her desk. Well, she used to have an attractive wicker wastepaper basket beneath her desk. She now she has a small pile of wet, chewed wicker. Either way, good on her for placing it within my reach.

In many ways, it's as if they have expressly organised the house to provide me with a variety of entertainment options.

For instance, they have a pantry with a door latch that doesn't quite work. By getting up on my hind legs and pushing hard with my front paws, I find it always opens. Inside there's all manner of stuff with which to while away a lazy ten minutes – a recycling crate to unpack, some Coles and Woolworths bags to rip to shreds, even a bag of treats which I'm in the process of learning to open.

There's also a park nearby where we go for a walk – this so I can 'interact' with other dogs. They vary in size and temperament but are pretty much always great fun. A slight problem: one of the humans, a park regular, arrives with what she calls a 'Great Dane'.

She clearly has been conned into buying a horse, thinking it's a dog. It's very sad. I want to say to her: 'Can you see the size of that thing? Have you ever actually heard it go "woof"? Why don't you invest in a saddle and give yourself a ride through the High Country?'

Whether this 'dog' comes from the same rip-off joint as the man's 'bicycle' I couldn't say.

The only real drama came a few days ago when I was suddenly a bit sick. I threw up my dinner and the lady ran around the house making phone calls and sounding upset, and then we all ran out and drove to the local vet who, after a thorough examination, declared that I was fine and not to worry. When I came home, I was allowed on the couch for the first time. The man and the lady sat on either side of me for hours, whispering my name and patting me and telling me what a good dog I was. My only achievement, I remind you, was to have chucked up my dinner. And yet from the way they were carrying on you'd think I'd just solved Fermat's Last Theorem.

Mum and Dad, I know there's a lot training ahead when it comes to these two. I'll just have to get stuck in.

Love,
Clancy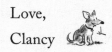

This first letter was composed when Clancy was still very young. I think it shows a certain lack of maturity. For instance, the way he criticises my use of the exercise bike. I'd managed to acquire the exercise bike free of charge, picking the ancient, rusted device from the council clean-up. I used it about three times, and then left it abandoned on the back porch, until the next council clean-up, at which point I heaved it back down onto the nature strip. Some other optimist then picked it up, and dragged it home, before throwing it out in a subsequent council clean-up.

Whatever Clancy's doubts, the bike has thus provided excellent exercise opportunities for the whole neighbourhood.

Age: **Five months**

C/- The Training Institute

Chateau Chaos

13 January

Dear Mum and Dad,

It's Clancy, your puppy, writing again from my new home in the city. Things are going well, even though I'm still trying to understand the human couple with whom I share the house. The couple have a well-provisioned fridge which they open all the time for their own benefit, but rarely for mine. Prior to the moment they open the fridge, I'm usually 'dozing like a baby' – to use their customary phrase. More accurately, I'm catatonic from lack of food.

Anyway, I jump up, exhausting the few calories I have left, and stand, wagging my tail with the last ounce of energy I possess, looking up hopefully as the man peers into the fridge. (I should mention that it's nearly always the man who peers into the fridge.)

The man then looks down, pats my head and says, 'You've already had *your* dinner,' which is fine if your definition of dinner is a handful of chicken scraps and a bowl of puppy milk.

This chap, I must point out, already has consumed *his* dinner, plus *his* dessert, and is now following up with – who's counting? Oh, I am – *his* third beer, but, in this bizarre system of bookkeeping, it's me who is accused of being a glutton.

And yet, as mentioned in my last letter, they are both nice people. The lady, whom I've taken to calling Lady, is very free with praise of me – much of it richly deserved. And the man, whom I've taken to calling Man, has composed a quite charming song, which he sings whenever I run towards him, the title of which is 'Clancy the Flying Dog'. The lyrics involve repeating 'It's Clancy the Flying Dog' followed by

where he lands no one knows,
since no one knows where he takes off,
because he's Clancy the Flying Dog

It's a song which, I am sure, would reach a larger audience if placed in the hands of a composer with a basic grip of rhyme, metre or melody. As well as with a singer who can hold a tune. Charming through he thinks it, I doubt it will trouble the judges at this year's Grammys.

Despite their enthusiasm for my presence in the household, both Lady and Man behave as if I am governed by different rules

Tricks

from those pertaining to themselves. For a start, much of the time, I have to do tricks in order to earn my food. Who would have imagined? Pardon me, but I thought the provision of basic food and lodgings was part of the deal.

'He *likes* doing tricks for his food,' Lady says, as if I'm a circus performer accustomed to passing around the hat each time I complete a somersault. Presumably she sees herself at the front of the dress circle, throwing a few coins on the stage. On the other hand, lest I sound whingey, it's true that I invented most of the tricks myself. Here's how it goes: I do something random, they give me food and invent a name for the trick, and so I do it again. As an example, I spin around – and then *after I've done it* – they sound the command, 'Around,' and start congratulating themselves for training me so well. Then I sit, *after which* they say, 'Sit.' Then I go totally down on the floor, *after which* they say, 'Go down.' Then I roll over *after which* they say, 'Roll over.' At this point, the chicken pieces rain down towards me as if from a hosepipe.

Occasionally Lady places some chicken on the ground in front of me and says, 'Leave it,' rewarding me with a different piece of chicken if I obey this frankly bewildering request. I'd like to see how she'd go putting a big cold glass of frothing beer in front of Man and saying, 'Leave it.'

All the same, food is not the only fun in life. The one thing that really excites them is when I take a book off the bookshelf and run with it out into the garden, chewing it up as I go. It is such good sport, creating a real carnival atmosphere. Both Lady and Man, if I can judge from their enthusiastic participation, love this game beyond all others.

We were playing it only the other day – Man chasing me around and around the garden, yelling, 'Clancy stop, Clancy come here!' –

while Lady kept screaming, 'Not the Wallace Stegner!' Lady has lots of books but it was this particular volume that seemed to get her attention. 'Oh, God,' she yelled from the back door, 'it's my favourite novel of all time.' At this point, I wondered whether I should learn to read, just so I could seek out other books by this author who appears to have so thoroughly won Lady's admiration.

In return for all this fun, I need to give something back. Whenever they are out of the house, I set to on the diggings. Perhaps you are aware of gold-digging districts such as Ballarat and Hill End. It is the can-do spirit of those old miners which inspires me.

Who knows what I could locate beneath the dirt of this suburban backyard? Man and Lady might come back one day after work and find that I've discovered a perfectly profitable iron ore deposit. Or that the backyard is now the site of a working coal-seam-gas operation, with me standing there in a hard hat, directing operations. Or that I've dug a new trade route to China.

If so – as they count their millions – I merely hope that Man and Lady might supply what I so fervently desire: an adequate serve of dinner.

From the city,

Much love,

Clancy

He's right about the Wallace Stegner. Our house is full of paperback books, many of them quite poorly written. Often by ourselves. So, by what mysterious process does a puppy always choose to chew the best pair of shoes, the most valued photo album, or the most treasured book? In his letters home, Clancy always seems full of grand questions about human behaviour, but so few about his own.

Age: **Seven months**

C/- The Training Institute

Chateau Chaos

13 March

Dear Mum and Dad,

I'm still working hard to train my humans, even though they seem incapable of the simplest of tricks. As an example, I've been trying to instigate a system whereby they take treats to the park – little bits of cheese or chicken – in order that I can

Agility training

receive some sustenance while I play. The deal is pretty simple: four times in a row, I come when summoned, am supplied a treat, and then resume playing with my good friends Lucky, Watto and Dougal.

On the fifth occasion, when everyone's keen to go home, I return for the treat and allow myself to be 'captured'. All good fun, and clever Clancy is five bits of chicken up on the deal. This worked perfectly for ten days in a row, then suddenly my humans entirely forgot how the game worked. Man and Lady came to the park with nothing. It was as if I'd never trained them in the first place.

Naturally, to underline the seriousness of the situation, I refused to be caught at the end of the play session, maintaining my customary work rate, with Man running after me, him waving his hands, begging, pleading, shouting, 'I have to go to work now, I'm going to be late,' me darting this way and that, like a footballer sidestepping his opponents, Man getting more hysterical, the other dogs and other humans watching the exhibition with immense amusement. Really, you could have sold tickets.

It was tiring, yes, but the effort was worth it. The next day, I'm delighted to report, the treats were back on the menu, which proves the adage: if you put the time into properly training your human, you do end up with a happy and loyal companion for life.

Hilariously, Man, in particular, has developed the idea that *he* is training *me*. In the backyard at home, he has constructed a hurdle, about half-a-metre high, by resting a piece of timber between two wooden boxes out in the middle of the grass. He stands on the far side with a bit of chicken in his hand and encourages me to come and grab the food. But by what route? I look at him, my big ears swivelling from side to side, trying to understand what he expects. Sometimes it's impossible to guess what's going on in his tiny brain.

I consider the question: is this intended as a test of agility or a test of intelligence. If it's a test of agility, he may want me to jump *over* the piece of timber. I prefer, however, to assume that it's a test of intelligence, and that he wants me to assess the optimal route between myself and the chicken. That's easy. It's the route which involves me running *under* the piece of timber.

I do so, expecting Man to give me undying admiration and, frankly, a bit of chicken. Bafflingly, Man seems unimpressed and refuses to hand over the treat. He looks fed up, even when I repeat the trick another twenty times – running *under* the timber each time; never jumping *over* the timber as that would be a sign of stupidity.

Thank God, I have him trained up to give me treats in the park or I'd be starving.

Until next time,

Love,

Clancy

I had wondered why the agility course proved such a failure. Clancy claims my intentions were unclear, and yet – as usual – he doesn't provide the reader with all the facts. For example: I not only provided verbal instruction of what was required, I provided a physical demonstration – constantly leaping over the barrier myself, first one way, and then the other, laughing and whooping in order to indicate what fun it was. Since Clancy clearly didn't see my display as instructional in purpose, I do wonder what he imagined I was up to?

Age: Seven months

C/- The Training Institute
Crumbling Manor
20 March

Dear Mum and Dad,

I have another problem requiring your advice. How do you get your humans up and out of bed in the morning? The park, after all, is not going to play with itself. On most mornings, Lucky, Watto and Dougal are already there when we arrive: I've missed out on half the party. Sometimes we're so late, they've already gone home.

That's right. No Lucky. No Watto. No Dougal.

Don't get me wrong: I know how to make my humans wake up. I let rip with a few barks and then just launch myself onto the bed, flying on my usual low trajectory so as to be able to land directly on Man's head. At this point, Man utters his usual out-of-date historical reference, like 'What do you think this is, the bombing of Dresden?' as if I spend all my spare time watching the History Channel. (Actually, I do. But he doesn't know that.)

Dawn Chorus.

Lady then scratches my ears, while Man makes tea and fetches the newspaper. They then sit in the bed and read the damn thing for, like, three days, as if they are unable to go out into the world without first knowing the winner of the Chess Olympiad, or what the political correspondent thinks about constitutional reform. I mean, who cares? Where's the chicken in that?

I try to get this message across by ripping to shreds any parts of the accursed newspaper that are not gripped tightly enough. I then use my right paw to bat the news section out of Man's hand. Save for typing out my demands and having them delivered to the front door by an armed sheriff, I fail to see how

I could make my point any clearer: 'The time to visit the park is NOW.'

Anyway, I must sign off. Man has again placed the piece of timber onto the boxes. This is the second week on a row. With a bit more effort, I may be able to teach him the rules of his own game.

Love,
Clancy

The jumping lessons again proved a disaster. They were permanently abandoned soon after. Clancy seems unwilling to jump, unless it's onto the back of an actual sheep.

Age: **Nine months**

C/- Chateau Chaos
15 May

Dear Mum and Dad,

A small scene from this morning.

Man says to Lady: 'I'm going to fill up the car and pick up some milk. I bet Clancy would like to come for the expedition.'

Lady smiles with delight. 'Oh yes!' she says, 'Clancy loves an expedition!'

I hear this all the time. Frankly, no thanks. The car makes me queasy. Just because I show some restraint in the chunder department, doesn't mean I enjoy vehicular transportation.

Besides, I do question the use of the term 'expedition'. Mawson's exploration of Antarctica? Edmund Hillary, Tenzing Norgay and the ascent of Everest? Sure, fine: these are expeditions.

Filling up the family station wagon at the nearest servo which accepts a Woolworths card? Speaking for myself: not an 'expedition'.

People assume that because one dog likes a particular activity, they all will. Some dogs chase balls; I don't see the point. Some dogs like car trips; others find them tiresome. Assisting a human when they are sweeping the house is, on the other hand, one of my favourite pastimes. What a delight to run around their feet, before performing a merry dance in what, moments ago, was a tidy pile of dust and dog hair.

Will write again soon.

Love,

Clancy

Fair point. I've always wondered why he lies down in the back-seat footwell, his paws holding closed his own mouth.

Age: **Ten months**

C/- The Diggings
Chateau Chaos
25 June

Dear Mum and Dad,

It's Clancy again, still trying to understand the mysteries of city life. For a start, the people I live with don't appear to have any useful occupations. I've forensically examined the backyard and can find no signs of sheep. They don't seem to have any crops either, unless you count a single pot filled with half-dead basil. And yet they act as if they are frantically busy, running around the house, then pounding on their computers, then charging around again, before collapsing on the couch and saying, 'Oh, God I'm exhausted.' During all this time, they have neither caught nor shorn a single sheep. The way they carry on, you'd think they were operating an outback station five times the size of Belgium.

Recently, I resolved to follow Man around the house, just to see if he ever does anything of interest. I get close to Man's legs and trail after him wherever he goes: up the hallway, into his bedroom, picking up a dirty coffee cup, then down the hallway to the kitchen, where he grabs a phone bill that needs paying, then it's up the hallway again to where he pays the bill, then down the hallway again to put new ink cartridges in Lady's printer.

I'm alert through all this, of course – nose sniffing, eyes shining, weaving around his legs so as not to miss a moment – and thinking: 'There must be a point at which he'll do something productive,' but that moment never arrives. If Man's life involves anything of even remote interest, then he's concealing it very well.

While Man and Lady dither around, achieving zero, I'm flat-out hectic. First there are my friends at the park – Lucky, Archie, Watto and Dougal. We tend to meet twice a day – early morning and early evening – although the five of us have to keep an eye on the clock, hustling our humans out the door, otherwise we turn up at different times, and where's the party in that?

Second up, there's the garden. My search for oil and gas reserves is going incredibly well. I've dug a series of test wells at regular intervals in the back lawn, to a variety of depths, most of the dirt kicked to one side so it's on the brick paving and thus away from the worksite. While none of the wells has yet proved commercially successful, some of the deeper holes may yet be found to contain iron ore. They just need a little more work. In the meantime, following the recent rains, they have provided the house with an attractive water feature.

As a sideline, I've found the holes provide a useful place to bury treasure, including the television remote control I purloined the other night. I plan to dig it up in a few months' time and present it to Man and Lady as a small token of my affection. In the meantime, I suppose I should thank the manufacturer for creating a device so small and easily portable, as if expressly designed for transportation by a dog.

Inside the house, there's much to be done. I've decided to start training for any kelpie agility trials that might be coming up. Man has decommissioned the jumping barriers previously installed in the backyard, so I'm making do with the furniture. By running incredibly fast up the hallway, I can launch myself towards the couch, achieving take-off much like a plane on a runway, thence to fly some metres on an upwards trajectory. I can then land either on the back of the couch or directly on Man's head, which at least provides Man and Lady with some entertainment – a useful thing now they can no longer operate the TV.

Once my flying missions are complete, I go and stand at the back door. I do this because Man and Lady always make a big fuss of me when I stand at the back door, so I assume they like me doing it. As always, it works: Man jumps up, wanders over to me, pats me on my head, and then opens the door.

I look up at him quizzically, wondering why he's opened the back door. Why would I want to go out there? It's winter, or hasn't he noticed?

'Oh, Clancy do make your mind up,' he says, and rather grumpily returns to the couch, where they are both continue to watch the blank TV screen.

If they don't want me to stand by the back door, why do they reward me so effusively when I do so? Why do they rush over and pat me, if – according to them – I'm doing the wrong thing?

As always, the secret lies in more training.

Love,

Clancy

So that's what happened to the remote.

Age: **One year and two months**

C/- Chateau Chaos

19 October

Dear Mum and Dad,

I write with some good news. Down at the park, I've met another kelpie, one called TicTac. He is such a fast runner it's hard not to be impressed. I think I'm better at the cornering, though he may beg to differ. We play a game we call Chasey Chasey, making up the rules as we go. The game is such fun that I think we should copyright it. I'm sure other dogs would be interested.

Some days I think TicTac is my best friend, but the very next day, I turn up to the park to find that Lucky is already there, or perhaps Watto or Archie or Dougal, and I change my mind about who is my very best best friend. Main thing, they are all great lads, and I include Dougal, who, counterintuitively, is a girl.

Certainly, the days go by in a blur. Before I left the countryside, I remember hearing people say, 'In the city, there'll be nothing for a kelpie to do,' but that's not true. As it happens, the park comes complete with a herd of small fluffy sheep, who require my

city jobs for country dogs

constant attention. They are the sort of sheep that go, 'Yap, yap, woof, woof' when I round them up, which is weird for sheep, but I don't like to judge.

At the house owned by Man and Lady, things are slightly more problematic. There's a pink crate in the corner of the kitchen into which Man and Lady throw a regular supply of intriguing plastic items. For instance, there's the plastic bottle from which they poured the milk, and the plastic box which contained the strawberries. As soon as they throw the items into the box it's game on. I fish each one out of the pink box – milk bottle, strawberry box, old tomato sauce container – drag them onto Man's bed and, while sitting atop his white sheets, rip the damn things into tiny, miserable shreds.

I think the contemporary term for this activity is 'imaginative re-use'.

Yet, despite this 'make-do' attitude on my part – creatively turning a piece of junk into a brilliant toy – their reaction is to run around, waving their arms, saying, 'No, no Clancy, that's ours, that's not for you.'

Then later: 'Oh, no! Look what he's done to the sheets!'

Well, if the crate isn't for toys, don't paint it pink, mate, that's my advice to you.

The other dilemma comes at night. When I was a little pup, living in the country, I slept in a zip-up kennel. I actually quite liked it. When I first arrived in the city: same deal, a big cube with fabric sides, zipped up so it felt safe, parked in the corner of Man and Lady's bedroom.

What happened next may be my fault. One night I had a nightmare – don't ask me what it was about! Probably a world-wide shortage of chicken! – and so Man unzipped the kennel and let me sleep on the bottom of the bed. That was fine, but on subsequent nights, I became concerned about the amount of activity in the street outside. I was trying to do a good job, you understand, in terms of home security. So, I'd sleep for a while on the bottom of the bed, then jump up and patrol the house.

Okay, it's true: they have wooden floors. Don't blame me, but I'm a young dog and the nails on my paws grow at a prodigious rate. Clip them as much as you like and – late at night, as I walk up and down – it will sound like the Queen's Household Cavalry doing manoeuvres five centimetres from a person's left ear hole. In fact, hurtfully, this is exactly what Man shouted out one night: 'It sounds like the Queen's Household Cavalry doing manoeuvres five centimetres from my left ear hole.'

I'll say it again: hurtful. Especially as I was only trying to make them safe. If someone broke in and robbed the joint, what's the bet it would be all: 'Why didn't Clancy wake up? Why was Clancy just snoozing away?'

So, long story short, now I'm back in the zip-up kennel, parked in the corner of Man and Lady's bedroom. Actually, it has zips on all sides, and sometimes Man forgets to completely seal one, so – by inserting my nose into the gap – I can extend the gap, slip out of the kennel, and – when morning dawns – find myself sleeping in a tiny circle at the foot of their bed.

'How did you get out?' Man asks, genuinely mystified.

I hope he never discovers my exit point. Actually, tomorrow I'm thinking of sticking up a poster of Rita Hayworth to disguise the already open hole. I saw this method used the other night when I was watching a film on the TV. I believe it was called *The Shawshank Redemption.* Maybe you've seen it?

Hope you are well. Despite it all, I'd have to say I'm flourishing.

Love,

Clancy

One day, I'll explain to Clancy that just because an animal has white fur, it doesn't mean it's a sheep. As for The Shawshank Redemption, *how is he watching this stuff? Especially now we no longer have a remote.*

Age: **One year and three months**

C/- Chateau Chaos

15 November

Dear Mum and Dad,

I caught a fly today. It seems worth a letter home. I've been snapping at them non-stop for months, without success. It had become an *idée fixe*, an obsession, a sickness of the mind. Now, I've caught one, I wonder what my obsession was all about. I'd been told that most wild game tastes like chicken. That is not true of fly. Fly, I've discovered, tastes like fly.

Love,

Clancy

PS: I rate this as my first major disappointment in life. Hopefully there are not many more ahead.

PPS: At least not of this magnitude.

What did he expect? I've swallowed plenty of flies and none of them were any good.

Age: **One year and five months**

C/- Onion Weed Cottage
29 January

Dear Mum and Dad,

Clancy here. I'm having a great summer; the only problem is the heat. A lot of the other dogs from the park go home to air-conditioning. Not us. When Man and Lady put me back on the lead, we walk up the hill and into a sauna. The heat is unbelievable. You wouldn't be surprised if, halfway up the hallway, there were ten nude Swedish men sitting on towels.

Usually, as soon as we open the front door, Man and Lady start to fight about the temperature inside the house. Man says we have no air-conditioning because he's 'an active environmentalist who cares about the planet'. Lady says we have no air-conditioning because he's 'a pathetic tight arse who, if he ever took his wallet out of his pocket, moths would fly out.'

This, at first blush, seems a little harsh, but I do notice that when she gives me dinner there are three lumps of chicken and when he gives me dinner there are two.

Anyway, once we get home, I usually collapse right there in the

front hall, going down with a bang, as if my legs have suddenly given way beneath me. I know dogs shouldn't take sides in any matrimonial disagreements, but the way I collapse, as if shot by a sniper, hopefully adds weight to Lady's case for the introduction of some form of cooling.

'Look at Clancy,' she always says. 'The poor dog is nearly dead from the heat.'

At this point – and they have this argument every day – he says, 'What rubbish. He's a kelpie. Kelpies love the heat. They were bred to run around the sheep yards in Dubbo.'

Yeah, right. As if Man has ever been to a Dubbo sheep paddock in his life. I feel like saying: 'Mate, that's dry heat. No one minds a bit of dry heat. It's this Sydney humidity that's the problem.'

You'd be proud, though. I say nothing. Frankly, I'm too busy panting.

Lady then does her speech about the house and its location. 'I think someone has mistakenly built this house directly over the open mouth of hell. I feel like a rotisserie chook. And it has zero air flow.' She then looks despairingly at Man, who merely pats at his own forehead with a tissue and says, 'Oh, it's not so bad.'

Not so bad! There is something weird about the house. It's located in a heat sink. You walk up the street and it's, like, 35 degrees, 35 degrees, 35 degrees, and then into the front yard – bang – 45 in the shade. Inside it's worse. Even the Swedish guys in towels would be finding it hot.

On this particular occasion, Man and Lady walked up the hallway towards the kitchen, still bickering. I heaved myself onto my four legs and followed them. Frankly, I always follow them, just in case something interesting happens. It never does. Except this time. Lady went into her office, turned on her computer and sat down to work. Sweat was flowing off her like a river off a cliff. It was basically like watching Niagara Falls. Then she began crying.

I moved close to her feet, looking up with my big eyes. (It's vain, I know, to comment on one's own physical attributes, but I have it on the authority of Lady herself that my eyes are 'the most beautiful in the world'.) Anyway, Lady is weeping at her keyboard while her loyal dog stares up in sympathy. Now, I'm not that familiar with the works of the Dutch masters, as dogs are not afforded entry to any of the major art galleries, but I think this scene would have repaid their attention. If Vermeer or Frans Hals had captured that moment, it would surely be the most popular postcard at the art gallery shop.

As it was, Man rushed in, all concerned and apologetic. It was no longer climate change this and climate change that. Suddenly it was, 'Oh, no,' and 'Are you all right?' And then, 'How about I go to Bing Lee right now?'

Long story short, he raced away in the car and returned with a portable air-conditioner – a machine for which Lady rapidly created the nick-name Odin, after the Norse God who delivers the icy winds from The North. You have to stick this tube out the window, which means you can't lock or even close the window, but Lady says, 'I don't care. I don't care at all. If I get killed in my bed by a knife-wielding intruder, at least I'll be cool at the time of death.'

During the day, the machine is set up in Lady's office and we sit there together, just me and her, enjoying everything the appliance can offer. Basically, we worship at Odin's feet. As the cool breeze ruffles my fur, I look up at Lady. She says, as she always says, 'Clancy, what beautiful big eyes.'

Actually, they are mainly wide with wonder. She got Man to spend $679, with as little as three minutes' crying.

Love,
Clancy

Yeah, yeah, very funny. What Clancy recounts as an amusing tale of a tightwad in retreat, I see as a case of a well-meaning man being unfairly manipulated. What's infuriating is the use of the word 'tightwad'. Clancy says 'tightwad' as if it were a bad thing. And yet when I hear the word I perceive the singing of angels. In particular, I see a person keen to save money, so he might spend it on something important – like chicken for his dog. Providing that dog doesn't keep using the term 'tightwad'.

Age: **One year and eight months**

C/- The Rented Hovel

28 April

Dear Mum and Dad,

Man and Lady have been renovating our normal house, so we've been living in what they took to calling 'the rented hovel'. Actually, it didn't seem so bad to me, but the backyard was pathetic and it was miles from the dog park. Some days, I missed seeing my mates Lucky, Gus and Pepper, which was pretty grim. This week, though, we moved back to our regular place. My God, Man made a meal of it. Give him a box of books to carry down a flight of steps, and it's all huff-huff, puff-puff and whingeing about the state of his knees. I tried to help as best I could, running in front of him, occasionally around him, as he made his way up the path – just ensuring it was clear – but all I received for my efforts was a harsh tone.

'Out of the way, Clancy.' And: 'Stop being a nuisance, Clancy.'

I'd have gone off and sulked except the next item to be carried out was my kennel, which Man said was 'far too heavy to lift', so he insisted on dragging it down the stairs, thump, thump, thump.

'Steady on, mate,' I thought. 'Someone's got to live in that thing once you've finished with it.'

Lady, meanwhile, just heaved things up on one shoulder and got on with it.

After we drove the furniture back to the regular house, we returned to clean the rented hovel. Man and I tackled the backyard. During our couple of months in the place, I'd done my best to extend the garden – digging up the soil and bark chips from the small flower beds and spreading them over the paved areas. It took a lot of work – a real daily effort on my part – and I'd managed to triple the size of the garden. Not only had I received little thanks, Man now seemed intent on reversing all my territorial gains. I couldn't understand it. Why not hand it back to the real estate agent with the improvements in place?

We travelled together to Bunnings – Man driving, me on the passenger seat with the breeze on my muzzle – while Man muttered about the garden and how it would be my fault if we didn't get our bond back. Once we got there, Man bought five bags of bark chips, plus a sausage sandwich. On the way back, I sat next to him in the car while he ate the sausage sandwich and lectured me about the price of the bark.

'Ten dollars a bag, Clancy, that's $50 for five bags, just to cover up your crimes.'

'Crimes?' I thought. 'Pardon? You wouldn't say that to Capability Brown.'

He also didn't give me any of the sausage.

Back at the house, Man methodically destroyed all my good work and shrank the garden back to its previous modest proportions. I did my best to subvert him, running around in circles, grabbing the broom with my teeth, and kicking up some of the bark as soon as he spread it.

Again, nothing but harsh words.

While he worked, he mentioned the price of the bark several more times. If you ever want to know the price of bark at Bunnings, just ask me, because I now have it memorised for life.

After my gardening efforts had been destroyed, we moved inside, and Man spent the next three hours cleaning venetian blinds. 'This is the worst job ever,' he said. 'What idiot would install venetian blinds? The only way to clean them is to do them individually, slat by slat.' He was spending far more energy talking about cleaning the venetian blinds than actually doing it. Meanwhile, Lady did the skirting boards – scrubbing away on her hands and knees without a word of complaint. I was pleased to be able to encourage her labours by giving her the occasional kiss.

After a million hours of this, we finally finished and drove to the real estate agent. Lady and I waited in the car, while Man dropped off the keys. He came back in an emotional state.

'They say that because we have a dog, we have to pay for a steam clean of all the carpets. Also, we have to have a pest company come in and check for fleas. It's going to cost nearly $500.'

He leant towards the back seat and gave my head a scratch. 'As if Clancy would ever have fleas. He's the most perfect dog in the world.' After all the friction between us during the day, finally I felt a moment of affection.

Back at our regular home, Man put me on the lead, and the three of us wandered down the hill. We were headed for the dog park. I was almost certain my friends would be there. And, you know what? They were.

Until next time,

Love,

Clancy

It took months for Clancy to forgive me for not handing over that bit of sausage.

Age: **One year and ten months**

C/- Chateau Chaos

15 June

Dear Mum and Dad,

It's Clancy here, writing home with exciting news from the city. There's finally some farming work on offer. Well, as close as it gets to farming in the big smoke. Man is cleaning up the backyard. He has a very noisy hand-held hedging machine. He turns it on and really attacks the hedge. By the time he stops, the hedge is virtually a stump. He then makes this speech. He says, 'I can't control my kids, I can't control my dog, but at least I can control my hedge.'

He shouts this out to Lady, who is reading the newspaper. Lady pretends to laugh, and then Man massacres another hedge. After he finishes the second one, he makes his little speech again: 'I can't control my kids …' etcetera – but this time Lady doesn't even pretend to laugh. Even I find it pretty repetitive, and Man is one of my best friends. Well, after Lucky, Watto and Pepper, and pretty much level-pegging with Dougal.

I try to help while the hedging is underway by running around Man in circles, jumping up in the air and snapping my teeth. It's my way of adding a festive atmosphere to the proceedings. Then, after he's finishing cutting, we have to bundle up all the trimmings so they can be thrown out during council clean-up.

Man says, 'We have to make maximum use of the council clean-up. It's the only free thing you ever get from paying your rates.'

He calls this out to Lady, but she's still busy with the newspaper, and doesn't seem to share Man's intense interest in the utilisation of free government services.

Man then cuts a length of thick twine and lays it on the ground. He stacks the trimmed branches neatly on top of the twine and kneels down in order to tie a slip knot. While he's down at ground level, I take the chance to lick his face a few times, wagging my tail and nuzzling his cheek, just to show how much I appreciate his move into agricultural work. I figure that if I'm sufficiently enthusiastic he might acquire a small flock of sheep, as I'd quite like to co-partner with him in our own business.

Anyway, Man pulls tight the rope and starts to compress the large bundle of clippings. I jump on top of the bundle and wriggle around. I'm only twenty kilos, but every bit helps.

He says: 'That's not helping Clancy,' which I really don't understand, as the rules of gravity indicate that my weight must be of some assistance in terms of achieving the compression required.

We do two more bundles and, each time, I jump on top just as he's pulling tight the rope. And each time, I'm given this entirely erroneous guidance about the downward pressure being of negative assistance. It's one of those times in life when you must embrace what you know is right, whatever others are saying.

Some considerable time later, we place the bundles on the nature strip and then head inside for a nice drink of water. Then it's back into the garden. A pile of compost needs to be added to the garden beds – a mixture of cow poo, chicken poo and other fertilisers. Man cuts open the bags and pours them onto the garden beds, at which point I run around in the stuff in order to spread it. It's real teamwork. I love it. Occasionally, Man says: 'Oh, Clancy,' but I'm guessing he's just expressing delight in my work ethic. In fact, I'm impressed with myself. After half an hour, I am tuckered out and covered head to tail in compost. I don't think I've smelt this good for months – or been so exhausted.

It seems like a good moment to have a nice rest on something soft. I don't want to trouble Lady or Man, so I just slip inside and stomp around until I find a comfy spot on the couch.

Hope you are all well in the country. As you can see, city life is pretty good.

Love,
Clancy

Clancy's letters are sometimes a little over-egged, but this account is spot on. How one dog managed to get so much compost onto a single pale-coloured couch remains difficult to explain. On a hot day, you can still smell it.

Age: One year and eleven months

C/- Chateau Chaos

22 July

Dear Mum and Dad,

Here's a weird moment from today, just in case you are looking for a story from the city with which to amuse people back home.

I've just paused at the entry point of the kitchen. A new system has been introduced, under which I'm told I'm 'not allowed in the kitchen, not allowed in here at all'. If I back out of the kitchen, and then sit at the entry point, I'm given a treat. Actually, it's a delicious bit of dried liver.

Here's the hilarious bit. If I wait outside the kitchen – never straying into the forbidden territory – the treat is not supplied. I have to go into the kitchen, be told off and then back out. After that, I get the treat. I can only assume this is what they are trying to achieve, so I now make sure I go into the kitchen whenever possible, even when I have no interest in so doing.

Man and Lady are nice, but I fear they are not that bright.

Much of the world of training is like this: entirely baffling. I pay attention, I really do. I cock my head, I swivel my ears. I make it clear that I am eager for further explanation, but none is forthcoming. If the humans are working from a training manual, why doesn't the dog receive a copy? That way, at least, we could all be on the same page.

Love,
Clancy

We were just doing what the book said. Suppling a copy to the dog is not usually considered necessary. Besides which, since Clancy is so clever why doesn't he try writing a new training manual? That way he could start paying for his own chicken.

Age: **Two years**

C/- Chateau Chaos

15 August

Dear Mum and Dad,

Man and Lady are still fun to live with, although they're often baffled by the simplest of instructions. I'll explain the situation, in case you can offer some advice.

When you're a dog, as I'm sure you know, you have to put real effort into getting your message across. I have finally worked up a series of tableaux, which appear to be doing the trick. My favourite is the living sculpture I create each day before breakfast. It involves me sitting neatly, just outside the back door, front paws tidily together, my head raised in a way that could best be described as noble. If this sculpture had an art gallery sticker, it would read: *Best Dog in the World*.

I can hear Man and Lady in the kitchen as they prepare my breakfast. 'Oh, isn't he handsome,' coos Lady as she fetches the bits of chicken.

'He seems to be lost in some very deep thoughts,' says Man, measuring out a cup of kibble.

Both appear sufficiently entranced in a way that can only, one hopes, bring a bonus in the tucker department. And nearly always, it works.

For my evening sculpture, performed when Man and Lady are watching television, I've gone for something completely different. This one is called *There's Something Outside to Which I Must Urgently Attend* and involves me standing at the back door, much like an English Pointer, back straight, tail flexed, nose gesturing towards the great outdoors. I want to create the impression that a brace of grouse has just been shot from the air, landing in the dense heather up by the back fence. It is imperative that the birds be fetched with some speed.

You've never been to the city, so I probably should tell you that we don't have any grouse in our backyard. Nor is there any heather. Nor does Man have a gun, which is a bit weird. Still, the backyard beckons, especially when Man and Lady are watching interminable drama programs on television, all of which, to my eye, feature quite poor scripts, tricked-up by glossy camera work. Each to their own, I suppose. Myself, I'd rather spend half an hour with my nose in the compost heap than endure a moment more of this rubbish. Again, the sculpture works. The door is opened and out I go.

That's not the end of my repertoire. *Legs Akimbo* is a kinetic artwork in which I lie on my back, legs pawing the air as if I were riding a four-pedalled bicycle. If translated into English, its approximate meaning would be: 'This stomach isn't going to scratch itself.'

My piece *Dog in the Wild*, meanwhile, is less a living sculpture and more an excursion into the world of creative dance. It involves me walking around in a tight circle on the wooden floor, as if to flatten some non-existent grass, before collapsing into a prone

Rodin's Clancy

Michelangelo's
Clancy

Egyptian Clancy

Some sculptural poses.

position. My intention is to summon up the whole exciting and eventful history of the dog – including that time when we would guard the camps inhabited by early humans, sniffing out enemies or signalling the presence of game. Back then, bedtime required a tamping down of the local vegetation. To re-enact the ritual, even though the floor here is either carpeted or fashioned from wood, is to pay tribute to that long history.

Despite all this, Man and Lady often speak to me as if I'm some sort of simpleton. Only last night, Man was sitting on the couch, watching yet another show on 'Rubbish.com', as I call it. I tried to get interested, but the script involved female prisoners arguing over who gets to be each other's bunkmate. It was like Canadian children's television, but with gratuitous references to sex and drugs. Even Man needed to provide his brain with an additional task, and was top-and-tailing snow peas.

I put my nose close to the bowl – really out of simple interest as to their plans for dinner – which resulted in a rebuke.

'Oh, Clancy, that's not for you. They're snow peas anyway. It's not like they're chicken.' Man then wagged his finger as one might if correcting a human toddler.

'Yes,' I felt like replying, 'I'm perfectly aware of the difference between a piece of chicken and a snow pea. I think you'll find my sense of smell is somewhat keener than your own. Besides which,

I'm not the one spending four hours at a time watching Netflix when there's a perfectly good compost heap ready to provide all manner of interactive entertainment.'

That's what I could have said, but sometimes it's easier to keep one's thoughts to oneself. Instead, I circled three times and collapsed to the floor, leaving Man to his snow peas and witless viewing.

Some say it was we dogs, with our fine sense of smell, who allowed the early humans to shrink the size of their own noses, thus freeing the cranial space necessary for the development of the human brain. We would sniff out predators, while they focused on developing human intelligence.

It's a good theory. But, before it goes into the textbooks, I'd like to see some evidence that human intelligence, in the end, eventuated.

Love,
Clancy

While I don't accept the truth of everything in Clancy's letters home, I accept this: it's true he can smell the presence of chicken – usually at some distance.

Age: **Two years and two months**

C/- Chateau Chaos

21 October

Dear Mum and Dad,

Hope all is well on the farm. The main news here is an outbreak of vermin. I think it's the unseasonable heat. I missed out on the park this morning because Man was too busy stomping on cockroaches. It was very amusing to watch, as he became totally transfixed by the task – silent, tense, waiting to make his move; then a sudden blaze of activity. It was like watching some combination of Mikhail Baryshnikov and Shintaro the Samurai, with Man flying from one side of the kitchen to another, a glinting, flying machine of death.

There's also a pantry moth infestation, a possum in the roof of the shed, and a very annoying flock of ibis, who keep invading my lawn. In terms of this grand battle, Man does not appear to be winning. Some of the mice round here are so large they should beep when reversing.

Every time we leave the house, the vermin tighten their grip. Outside, magpies the size of small fighter jets swoop the barbecue, hoping for a dropped sausage. The mosquitoes sit behind a screen of bushes, rolling their large eyes, wondering how long it is till dusk. It's like life on the Serengeti after the first rains of the season. You half expect David Attenborough to emerge from behind the shrubbery.

One day, when we left for our walk, the kitchen floor featured eight scampering cockroaches. By the time we returned, there were 27 cockroaches, who appeared to have organised their bodies to spell out: 'We're Winning.'

Please send help.

Love,
Clancy

He's right. The cockroaches around here are ridiculous. They scurry around every time you put on the light. Actually 'scurry' is not the right word. It's more like the brisk, purposeful walk of a commuter on the way to work. I have tried traps, of course, which the cockroaches regard as mobile housing, dotted around for their convenience. I have tried insecticide, which had a worse effect on me than on them. Female cockroaches, I read online, can produce seven egg capsules in a lifetime, each holding as many as 48 eggs. How many is that? Just multiply 7 by 48, and you'll get the answer: 'Eeuw.'

As Clancy mentions, we also have a bad infestation of pantry moths, which I'm trying to kill with traps – essentially a sheet of sticky paper impregnated with female pheromones in order to attract the males. It's a sort of insect version of an Australian nightclub. The problem: 95 per cent of the males are killed, but the rest struggle free. It's these big, powerful ones that get to breed with the females. My pantry is now home to accelerated evolution. Leave it three weeks, and there will be three lion cubs living in there.

With his sheep-herding skills, I wonder why Clancy can't do more to help. Then again, maybe he's getting too much pleasure from seeing me leap around with a rolled-up magazine, trying to do my worst. If the Buddhists are right, and life is all about karma, I'll arrive in heaven only to have God smite me around the head with a copy of Good Weekend *and spray me with a good shot of Mortein.*

Age: **Two years and three months**

C/- Dog Park
20 November

Dear Mum and Dad,

Quick update. My friend Bella was at the park today, after a long absence. Apparently, her human owners, a delightful couple in their early twenties, split up some months ago. The young woman, the more engaging of the two, lost custody. Bella now spends most of her time in the swanky seaside suburbs. Erggh! The parks are inadequate, the dog treats are overpriced, and the beaches are closed to those of us with four legs. Still, Bella was in a good mood today, reunited as she was both with her old owner and, more importantly, with me.

When couples break up, why can't the dog choose with whom to live? Another human mystery for you to ponder.

In haste and with love,
Clancy

Fair point. There should be a Family Court for dogs.

Age: **Two years and four months**

C/- Chateau Chaos

15 December

Dear Mum and Dad,

I'm just back from the park! We've been away for the holidays, so I had a lot of messages to catch up on. There were trees I could have sniffed for an hour, but Man kept urging me on, saying, 'Come on, Clancy, we haven't got all day.' With some trees, I hardly had time to read the messages, never mind composing a proper reply.

Later on, I sat on the floor next to Man's desk while he caught up with his own messages, most of them from online wine suppliers who appear to believe they are on to a good thing. It took hours, with me just sitting there, yet not once did I say, 'Come on, Man, we haven't got all day.'

That's the thing with dogs and humans. The rules are different according to which species you happen to be.

I'm not complaining, but some things do grate. Most mornings, Lady takes me to the park to see my mates. Sometimes, we're running late, and arrive to see Pepper and her crew are already heading home. At this point, Lady says, 'You've missed your chance, Clancy. You should have been down here earlier.'

Argghhh. I assume she means this as some sort of humorous aside, but it's wearing thin, especially since she makes the comment at least twice a week. I feel like saying, 'Come on, Lady, how about working up some new material.'

The truth is that I am always up and ready for action at 6 am. It's Lady and Man who seem to think that a park visit can occur only after they have spent an interminable period lying in bed, going through every page of the newspaper, as if the whole country was dependent on them being abreast of world affairs. What do they imagine? That ASIS is going to turn up and say, 'We haven't had time to follow the situation in North Korea, can the two of you fill us in?'

True fact: through this whole process, I have to wait for my breakfast, even though I'm practically dead from starvation. Some days, I find myself hoping for world peace – partly for its own sake, but also to limit the news they need to get through. In the end, they finally put down the paper, supply my breakfast, and then we head to the park.

As we walk along, Lady talks to me almost constantly. She says, 'You are such a handsome dog,' and 'What a fine dog you are,' and

'You are so good the way you walk beside me,' all of which strike me as useful observations.

Then we see Pepper leaving the park and she does the bit about how it's my fault, as if I should be more aware of the clock. (Memo to Lady: I don't own one!)

Still, at least when Lady talks to me, I'm the one for whom the message is intended. Down at the park, I notice a lot of humans talk to their dogs but only as a means of communicating with other people. They say things like, 'I think that dog plays a little rough for you,' or 'The owner of that dog should put him on a leash, don't you think?' or 'Watch out for that cyclist, he's going way too fast.'

Why don't they address these messages to their intended recipients? What are we dogs meant to do? Translate the message into a series of barks? And why do humans seem to think that what they're saying is less aggressive if it's merely overheard by its intended recipient. Here's my point: if you have a problem with cyclists using the dog park, write a letter to the mayor. It's no good telling your dog. We don't get to vote in municipal elections.

It's even worse when humans take it upon themselves to speak as if they are the dog, putting words into our mouths. We'll finish the dinner in our bowl and they'll pretend to be us, saying something dumb like, 'Uh-oh, my dinner is all gone.' Shockingly, embarrassingly, they use what they imagine to be a doggy voice. 'Rug-roh, my rinner

is all rone.' I want to tell them, 'Look, my friend, Scooby-Doo was a cartoon character. He wasn't a real dog. He was voiced by an actor, don't you know, and a human one at that.'

If humans are going to create a dog voice, why does it have to include a speech impediment? Why, when people do a dog voice, do they puff up their cheeks and speak from deep in their throat? Do they not realise that this is a little unfair, particularly when it comes to one of the more intelligent breeds of dog, of which a kelpie might be the most obvious example?

Personally, if I bothered to speak, I'm sure my voice would emerge with a rich timbre, precise articulation, plus the rough warmth of the Australian bush. If someone wanted to impersonate my voice, I'd recommend an hour or two listening to Jack Thompson reciting the poems of Henry Lawson.

Meanwhile, it's nearly time for my afternoon trip to the park. I'm just hoping we pause by the tree near our driveway. I'm only halfway through the most recent message and am very keen to find out the full story.

Until next time,

Love,

Clancy

This is unfair. I always let him sniff every tree. Yes, I'm forced to give him the occasional hurry-up. But if I didn't give him a hurry-up, we'd be there all day. I know that his nose is sensitive; that he is decoding the smell of scores of dogs, then matching it to a database in his head, in order to identify who's been hanging out in the neighbourhood. It's very impressive. But does it need to happen every time we walk home from the park? It's like me going past a library and deciding I need to whip in and read every book, cover to cover. That urge to linger may be impressive, but does it fit in with the sort of regular employment that can result in the purchase of chicken?

Age: **Two years and five months**

C/- The Diggings

Chateau Chaos

14 January

Dear Mum and Dad,

You find me, with this letter, in a scientific frame of mind. I've always been taught that humans and dogs co-evolved over thousands of years. The job of the humans was to run the camp – providing food and so forth – while the job of the dog was to patrol the perimeter of the settlement and give warning of any impending threat. It's worked well for 30,000 years – which is why, at 6 am, I feel honour-bound to vigorously announce that a stranger is walking past the property.

I am responding to the deep call of our joint evolutionary history, but suddenly, it seems, there's a problem. There's no 'Thank you Clancy for drawing our attention to this possible threat.' No 'Good thing we have a dog willing to stay alert all night, always on task.'

It's all 'For God's sake, Clancy, it's only Gary, he's going to work. The guy has a right to go to work.'

Well, pardon me. They all seem to know this 'Gary', but I'm yet to have the pleasure of making this particular gentleman's acquaintance.

And what if I were to decide – unilaterally – that this 'Gary' posed no threat? What if this person, this 'Gary', turned out to be a real danger to the family? Well, frankly, it's more than my job's worth. If I have to face censure for being over-zealous, for working too hard, then so be it.

Besides which, between us, the man is definitely dodgy.

I continue to do good work in the backyard. I hear on the radio that the price of iron ore remains surprisingly resilient on China's Dalian Commodity Exchange – or the DCE, as it's commonly abbreviated by those in the know. This is good news for me, as I'm expanding my mining operations. I'm still trying to find a good lode of extractable ore. It's my view that Western Australia has dominated this trade for too long. What fun to give Gina Rinehart and Andrew 'Twiggy' Forrest a run for their money.

I've switched from deep wells, as I'd prefer to locate a lode close to the surface. This involves multiple shallow extractions, placed at one-metre intervals all over the property. Some are on grass, others in flower beds. Really it makes no difference. What's under the surface is the main thing.

So far, no iron ore has been discovered, but that just means more digging. I'm sure Lang Hancock didn't give up his ambitions after his initial glance at the Pilbara. 'If at first you don't succeed …'

Between my patrolling duties at night and my digging duties during the day, I'm pretty much fully occupied. Then again, as they say, the devil makes work for idle h . . . paws.

Very pleased to be so busy. Hope you are too.

Until next time,

Love,

Clancy

On legal advice, I'd like it noted that there is nothing dodgy about Gary.

Age: **Two years and six months**

C/- Chateau Chaos

21 February

Dear Mum and Dad,

It's hot. Damned hot. My tongue is hanging so far out of my mouth, I'm worried it might get tangled up in my feet. One upside of the heat, a lovely upside, is that we have been swimming. We drive to this river, a couple of hours from the city, and then jump in. We swim to the opposite bank, Man and I, my muzzle ploughing through the water, and then race back again. I always beat him. There's only one weird thing. After we get out and I shake myself down, both Lady and Man make such a fuss. It's 'Oh, what a clever dog,' and 'Oh, Clancy, you are so fast.' They make such a tedious song and dance about my swimming.

It's dogpaddle, people. The clue is in the name. If a dog can't dogpaddle, who can?

This is my main complaint about life in town. You have to wade through an endless sea of compliments. Everything I do, it's 'Good dog this,' and 'Good dog that.' It's as if they are worried about my self-esteem. I want to say: 'Really, I'm fine. I'm relaxed and confident about my abilities when it comes to being a dog.'

The other day, as I relieved myself on a tree, one of them even took the opportunity to observe: 'Now that's a big wee.' Really? Is urination now some sort of achievement? I notice they don't pay each other a compliment upon managing it – a good thing, too, since this would involve cheering on Man twice nightly as he gets up, potters along the hallway and then returns to bed.

It's not that I dislike all praise. Every morning, first thing, Lady tickles my ears, strokes my back and says, 'You are such a handsome dog,' which is factual enough. Objecting to it would be as foolish as complaining that someone has calculated two plus two and come up with four. All the same, back on the farm you hardly ever get praise. Round up 500 sheep on the hottest day of the year and it's 'Not a bad job.' That's it. Tickle under the chin if you're lucky. A few extra hours on the chain the next day, just so you can get a sleep in.

In the city, the praise comes without reason or cause. Being a dog, any sort of dog, is sufficient. A nose, two ears and four legs is enough to crack it. Actually, I know one dog who garners heaps of praise, even though you could count his legs without going past the number three.

Kids are the worst. Man and I go walking through the park

and every day there will be a small human, four or five years old, saying, all excited, 'Mum, Mum, look it's a dog!' Well, sure. Full marks for observation. I feel like making a fuss back, 'Hey, wow, look, it's a tiny human.'

I don't say anything, of course, as I'm busy playing with my friends Lucky, Watto and Archie. We circle and leap. We chase each other. Watto does a sharp turn. Dust flies. He's heading for the big tree as fast as a greyhound, Lucky and me in full pursuit. Round we all go, looping the big tree, a blur of fur, then sprinting back into the sunshine in the centre of the park.

The kid is still watching, standing there with his folks, eyes open wide. 'Dad, Dad,' he says, pulling on his father's hand, his voice full of wonder. 'Look at that *dog*.' Sure, it could have been a reference to one of the other dogs. We were all going too fast to see which of us he was pointing at. Still, when the kid said *'dog'*, I'm pretty sure he meant me.

It was a moment of clarity. The moment when I began to realise – here in the city – I need to moderate my attitude to compliments. Put on a good show and you should be willing to accept the audience's applause. That's my new principle. And so, after we'd finished our round of Chasey Chasey, I wandered over to the kid, still panting, and allowed him to stroke my fur as he sang my praises to his dad.

'Dad, did you see this dog? Did you see how fast he went? Did you see how amazing he is?'

Did I deserve such unrestrained acclaim? Not really. I'm a dog; other dogs could do it. Other kelpies, for instance.

By the way, the cockroach infestation continues. If I could find a way of herding cockroaches, that really would be something.

Love,
Clancy

What's wrong with praise? I dream of getting praise. I come from the generation in which parents and teachers would rather die than give anyone praise. There were two favourite phrases used when I was growing up: 'Don't get too big for your boots', and 'No one likes a big-noter'. One of these phrases, or more commonly both, would greet any achievement.

Child: 'Good news, Mum, I just got 99 out of 100 in English.'

Mum: 'Don't get too big for your boots, no one likes a big-noter, and I don't think the word "got" is very good English, so I'll be complaining to your teacher that you were given such an undeservedly high mark.'

Australia's humans operate what you might call a national 'bragging ban'. Not only are you not allowed to receive praise, you are certainly not allowed to compliment yourself. If one of our cricketers is paid a compliment, having thrashed the English and set a new world record, he is required, upon returning to his country, to stare at his own feet and bashfully mumble: 'I guess I wasn't too bad on the day.'

Similarly, an Australian scientist, upon winning the Nobel Prize, is called upon to observe: 'They must have been pretty desperate that year.'

I exaggerate, but only slightly.

We're a nation of under-estimators. It's the only place in the world where an atrocious act is described as 'a bit ordinary', while an act of genius is 'not half bad'. Where else in the world is your best friend described as 'a total bastard', whereas someone truly evil will be only 'a bit of a bastard'?

If I were Clancy, I'd accept whatever praise was going.

Age: **Two years and seven months**

Wallow Hollow
C/- Chateau Chaos
14 March

Dear Mum and Dad,

As the French say, 'Plus ça change, plus c'est la même chose' – 'The more things change, the more they stay the same'. Currently, I'm engaged in quite a battle with Man over the use of the garden. I've created a delightful wallowing area just near the back door. By removing the grass and excavating some of the dirt, I've fashioned a perfect Clancy-shaped hollow. I call it my Wallow Hollow. On a hot day, there's nothing better than feeling the dirt against your fur. I know it's counterintuitive, but a good wallow leaves me feeling cleaner. The dirt is like an exfoliation. Others prefer hot water and dog shampoo, but I think it's wrong to make a fetish out of cleanliness.

So far so good. But every time I do some excavations, Man seems to lose his will to live. He walks out the back, sees what I've done and breaks into the sort of keening that I associate with a funeral in ancient Rome. It's all woe, woe and thrice woe.

'Oh, Clancy', he says, as if I've just torn a hole in the Mona Lisa, 'what have you done? How will I get that grass to regrow?'

He then goes inside and dobs on me to Lady, which is frankly un-Australian. I stay outside. I can see him, waving around his hands, but I can't hear what he's saying, which may not be the world's most crushing deprivation.

Next, he's back, huffing and puffing. He marches around the garden and I can tell he's planning something. Sometimes, watching Man, you can virtually hear the gears in his brain, whirring around, trying to find purchase. Finally, he spots the outside table with its metal chairs. He grabs two of them and walks towards my Wallow Hollow, then places the chairs on top of my excavations. Why would someone want to do that? Not only is the ground uneven, leaving the chairs listing at strange angles, but I can no longer use my Wallow Hollow. An area of great utility has been ruined. It's like building a swimming pool and then putting bars over it.

'What are you doing, mate?' I think to myself. 'You are just creating more work for me.'

At this point Man and Lady leave for the afternoon, which is just as well, as I can work uninterrupted, creating a fresh Wallow Hollow from scratch. This time I choose a spot right outside the back door. Maybe it's a better spot anyway; more conveniently located. In the end, I'll be thanking Man for forcing me to relocate.

I get digging, sending dirt flying into the air and onto the path. It's hard work but I give it my all. Perhaps he'll approve if this Wallow Hollow is on a grander scale. Maybe the old one was too small for his taste. I dig solidly for the best part of the afternoon. I'm like a worker in a West Australian mining camp. I should be wearing hi-vis.

Just as I'm finished, I hear the car returning. I position myself in the new Wallow Hollow so they might appreciate how well it works and how elegant I look stretched out in the freshly dug soil. Man is first to spot me. As soon as he opens the door, we're back to the full Roman funeral. There's a performative aspect to the whole thing, as if he wants the entire neighbourhood to share in the horror he is experiencing.

'You've dug right outside the back door. I'll have to step over your hollow, just to get into the backyard. This is the worst place you could have chosen. It's wrecked the whole garden.'

I look up at him with the sweetest, most agreeable look I can manage, as if to say, 'If the excavations are not extensive enough, I'm willing to have another go.'

At this point, his shoulders sag, as if in defeat. 'Okay, Clancy,' he says. 'You win.' He lifts the metal chairs off the first wallow and places them on top of my new wallow.

He bends down to talk to me. He says, 'How about you let the grass grow back on this bit right outside the back door, and I'll agree not to interfere ever again with your original Wallow Hollow.'

Obviously: fine. I'm not an unreasonable housemate. But did I have to go through a whole afternoon of heavy-duty excavations just to get back to where we started?

And what about the rest of the garden? Down here in the city, the inhabitants have no sense of making use of the land. If it were me, I'd have a chook shed up the back – I could patrol the area myself – and two sheep to keep down the grass. Instead of which there are just three flower beds – useful as bone storage areas but not for much else.

It's all a mystery to me, and no doubt to you as well. I'm sure things are more sensibly arranged back home.

Until next time.

Love,

Clancy

Dogs, I realise as I flip though Clancy's letters home, have many lessons to teach us humans. Among them: life is not perfect, you cannot have everything you want and sometimes you have to compromise.

Clancy's Wallow Hollow is the perfect example. I would like a perfect back lawn, I really would. I would like a lawn without an unsightly patch of dirt in which dog toys are half-buried, dug up then buried afresh.

For a time, I thought I could have such a lawn. After all, it was growing well, all I had to do was to prevent Clancy from digging in that one spot. Hence the garden chairs, placed on top of his diggings, with the plan that this might allow the grass to recover.

But – and here comes the lesson – life is, at its core, sub-optimal. It cannot be perfect. It's why Turkish rug makers put a tiny flaw *into every rug – otherwise God would be offended at their assertion of human perfection. Clancy's Wallow Hollow was that knot in the Turkish rug of our backyard. I just had to learn to accept it. Many months later, it's still there: not growing, but also not shrinking.*

Clancy and I, well, we've reached an accommodation.

Age: **Two years and nine months**

C/- Crumbling Manor

20 May

Dear Mum and Dad,

Is it necessary for a dog to be a 'good host'? This was the phrase used by Man and Lady yesterday when a new dog came to our home. 'Clancy,' they said, 'you must be a good host.'

Here's what happened. The doorbell rang. I rushed up. The front door opened. Two humans and a dog were standing there. I gave the dog a good sniff, and … I had no memory of this animal. I have perfect nasal recall when it comes to dogs, and this particular mutt was not featured in my extensive database.

And yet here he was, bold as brass, coming into my hall, smelling my possessions, wagging his tail, and then accepting a scratch under the chin from Lady. What a liberty.

His name, apparently, is TJ and he comes from the Eastern Suburbs. Big deal. I don't care. I think he has a nerve. I made my displeasure clear. I may have growled in a slightly alarming way. I may have showed him what my teeth looked like, just in case he had an interest in taking up a career in dog dentistry.

So, what was the result of this alarming incursion into my home? It was I who received the rebuke! That tired line about being a 'good host'. Then there was some blather from Man and Lady about 'It's Michael and Jenny,' and 'TJ is their dog,' and 'Michael and Jenny are lovely,' all of which might be true, but where's the proof that this 'Michael and Jenny' have good taste when it comes to their choice of dog?

Worse, all this negative talk about yours truly was conducted in front of TJ. Oh, he was soaking it in, make no mistake. He was loving it. He was wagging his tail as if to say, 'Oh, I'm just a cute spoodle and isn't that Clancy terrible? Just look at that vicious out-of-control working dog, really he should be on a chain in some sort of dusty paddock.'

Talk about fake news. This so-called 'TJ' was a dog intent on drinking my water and stealing my stuff. If I were working for the tabloid press, I'd have a label for what he was up to: it was a home invasion.

I do realise that I'm sounding intolerant. Suspicious of the unfamiliar. Prejudiced towards those who enjoy a life of wealth, privilege and cool breezes in the much-admired Eastern Suburbs.

Well maybe. But two things to remember. He's not my friend. I issued no invitation. He just turned up with 'Michael and Jenny'.

Second thing: if this visitor was one of my friends, I would have behaved quite differently.

Imagine if Man and Lady had invited over the humans who are associates of Pepper or Archie or Gus, and that – as a result – I'd been able to show them my home.

Well, then I'd be all smiles. I'd be the one at the front door, pushing a welcome wagon full of treats. I'd be the one out the back, saying, magnanimously, 'Oh, please, dig up any bone you fancy.' Or 'Why not have a go at my water bowl?'

If it was Pepper – this is a bit personal – I'd even be willing to give her a go in my Wallow Hollow. I'm sure her owners, Lady and Lady, would cheer us on.

But this is different. This is war.

This is the Russians resisting the Germans at Stalingrad. This is the brave Spartans at Thermopylae. This is the Australians seeing off the Japanese on the Kokoda Track. I dislike bragging in any form, but – let's get real – this is the heroic story of one brave soldier on a mission to protect all he holds dear.

And yet, am I awarded a medal? I am not. Instead, it's criticism. 'Oh, Clancy you are such a terrible host.'

Here's my question: what is a 'good host'? In my book, a good host is someone who curates a gathering of like-minded individuals who might share a few convivial laughs. The clue is in the phrase 'like-minded'. The invitation list is crucial. It doesn't include the likes of TJ.

And for all their criticism of yours truly, I don't see Man and Lady just inviting anyone who might want to wander up their front steps.

'Hey, you', I don't hear them saying, 'I've never met you, but why don't you come in and smell all our stuff.'

I know the afternoon should have ended with me accepting TJ, and understanding my folly, and the two of us gambolling together in the backyard. It did not. I was placed in Man's bedroom, with the door closed, while various convivial food-based activities were enjoyed, involving Michael, Jenny and – yes – TJ. I could hear the sound of laughter, and of eating, through the firmly closed door.

Sometimes life is so unfair.

Yours, in hope of justice.

Love,

Clancy

I'm glad you, dear reader, have now experienced Clancy's darker side. I realise he believes that his behaviour is always faultless, but I think the careful student will see through the façade. In terms of literary genres,

I compare the above letter to The Remains of the Day, *by Kazuo Ishiguro. Much like Stevens, the deluded chronicler of that tale, Clancy is an unreliable narrator. I trust, reading the above, you will see through his self-delusions and spare a thought for all of us – including TJ, who really is a lovely chap.*

Age: **Two years and ten months**

C/- Crumbling Manor
22 June

Dear Mum and Dad,
Here's a phrase recently overheard at our place: 'Wouldn't you enjoy living the life of a dog? Look at Clancy, lying there in front of the couch – and not a thought in the world.'

The speaker, obviously, is Man. He often sprouts this sort of unscientific garbage. In his eyes I'm just lying there, blank to the world, twenty kilos of pure-bred Australian kelpie doing nothing that couldn't be achieved by a big bag of spuds.

It's so annoying when he says things like this. After all, get a scientist on the case and, oh, what a different picture would emerge.

Any decent dog researcher – Alexandra Horowitz is my personal favourite – would start by paying attention to my nose. To the unobservant person – for example, Man – I'm just 'lying there', but, if that's the case, why are my nostrils twitching? The truth? I'm bloody busy. According to Horowitz, my nose is sucking in air and then processing the information as part of a highly sophisticated process. The nose, when operated by a dog, is conducting a constant search of areas near and far – identifying interesting smells, then probing each smell for further information as to its location and age.

When was the smell created? Is it some weeks old or of more recent origin? How far away is it? Was it created by a known source, thus providing a crucial clue to understanding a previously opaque pattern of behaviour? Or is this evidence of an animal new to the district?

A dog's nose, you should understand, is designed quite differently from that of a human. As noted by Horowitz, the air can be held within the dog's nose for analysis, while fresh air is simultaneously brought into the test chamber, in a way that would defeat any human, with the possible exception of a didgeridoo virtuoso.

In any given moment, there's a lot of information coming in. An example: right now, Connie and Jim next door are having a barbecue, and I'm assessing what they are cooking for dinner. It's part of my concern for Lola, their very agreeable companion animal. Lola, with whom I commune via the fence, certainly deserves the odd titbit from their table. She's smart and, by my observation, extremely loyal. Now Jim, according to my analysis, is cooking lamb chops, but he's also just thrown on a handful of spicy sausages and – just a few minutes ago – added some sweet corn, steamed on the cooktop inside and then charred on the barbecue.

I feel like saying: 'Jim? What are you thinking? No one wants to live next to a trendy.' Only kidding. But if I were Lola, I'd be eschewing the corn and begging for the chops, which, from the evidence coming in, Jim has cooked to perfection.

More sniffing. Like a radar-detection system, my nose conducts an extensive search of the neighbourhood. Down the road, working late, Rosco, the local mechanic, is servicing a customer's car at the garage and is busy changing the oil. He's using a high-quality brand for the refill, which doesn't surprise me, as Rosco is a man of honour. If I had a car, which I don't as yet, Rosco would get all my business. Meanwhile, Jurate – across the road – is cooking dinner. Oh, my God. You should smell it. One plate of that tucker and I could die happy. Jurate is the best home cook in the world. I correct myself. She is the best home cook among those willing to offer me the occasional taste. If others want to enter the competition, they know where to find me.

Closer in, I can smell the chickpeas Lady is preparing for dinner. I can support most progressive causes, but I feel her embrace of two-days-a-week vegetarianism needs more discussion. The future of the planet is important, I get that, but if she and Man stayed home, instead of going on interstate holidays, they'd have enough carbon credits to afford a geyser of uninterrupted chicken.

I wriggle on the floor. My nose twitches, sucking in more information. Man is folding the laundry, which still smells of washing detergent and sunshine.

Again, Man makes an attempt at humour: 'You're lucky you just have your fur, Clancy. You never have to fold anything.'

This so hilarious that Lady rolls her eyes, while I distract myself by taking a huge sniff of my own paws. Oh, the smell is something. I can differentiate every grain of dirt from this afternoon's work on The Diggings. It's a rich loamy odour, with after-sniffs of my own doggy paws, from previous sessions of digging, perhaps even when I was still a puppy.

I find the whole sensation quite moving. In fact, if smells had promotional names, much like paint colours, this one would be called 'Achievement'. Or, maybe, 'A Nobel Success'. Or better, 'Heroic Persistence in the Face of Criticism by a Particular Person Who Appears Not to Understand the Productive Intent of The Diggings'.

Anyway, at this point Man leans down from the couch. He appears to have given up on the unscientific garbage about 'Clancy's just lying there'. Instead, he's quite tender and scratches me behind my ears. Whatever our disputes when it comes to The Diggings, fair go to Man, he really does know how to hit the sweet spot.

I give him a big sniff. Partly so he knows I love him. But also so I know what he's been up to since this morning. My finding, just in case you are interested: a totally boring and uneventful day! Does this person do anything interesting? I doubt it! His day is certainly not a patch on mine. No offence to Man, but, for a start, he has met no other dogs, not a single one, not even Lola (just next door!). Also: he has had no interaction with any lamb chops. (Hello? Jim is cooking them five metres away!) And he hasn't been in to have a chat to Rosco at the garage, who, he claims, is a friend.

I know Australian men are bad at this stuff, but it can't be that big an effort. Go in and have a sniff. Talk about the weather, ask about the kids. Do whatever, as a human, floats your boat.

The only good point is that there's been no drinking. Three weeks ago, I had a good sniff one night when Man came home late after 'stopping off at the shops'. I keep my findings to myself, but unless Woolworths has installed a keg, with a bowl of peanuts served as an accompaniment, there's more to this 'shopping' than is being admitted.

I'm not telling Lady, who, I happen to know, has her own secrets – secrets I remain unwilling to divulge.

Main point: we dogs know. We know everything. It's in the nose. Want a private detective? Hire us. Want a top-line spy?

Get yourself a dog. And, if you are human, never again look at your nose-twitching hound and think, 'Oh it must be nice to do nothing.'

Mum and Dad, I know you realise all this, but thank you for listening while a new generation of dogs is forced to publicise the bleeding obvious.

Love,
Clancy

I understand Clancy's point. People often accuse me of just lying around, doing nothing, when actually there's plenty going on. Yes, it looks as if I'm asleep on the couch, but my brain is active, whirring through the world's problems. Given sufficient time asleep, I should be able to solve nearly all of them.

Age: **Two years and eleven months**

C/– The Doghouse
Chateau Chaos
20 July

Dear Mum and Dad,

Again, I write from my house in the city. Well, when I say 'house', I mean doghouse, both literally and figuratively. All the talk here is of the Great Ham Incident and the continuing investigations into who took a giant bite out of the leg of ham when it was sitting, unguarded, in an Esky on the laundry floor.

Without making any admissions, it's true I was the only canine present at the time of the incursion.

There are some mitigating factors worth mentioning. Man was having a party for his birthday. Some of my favourite people were here, so I was expending a lot of energy, running up the hallway to greet family members, then out the back to check on the neighbours and friends who'd already arrived.

Herding sheep is so much easier than herding humans. One lot was in the kitchen; another mob was standing around the barbecue. For a dog with rounding-up instincts this is quite psychologically distressing. You want the whole party to be gathered in one place. Even more distracting, the fridge door was constantly being opened. Whenever the fridge door is operated, I like to investigate. I could be three rooms away, with loud music playing, but I can always hear the swing of that door.

In the normal course of affairs – on, say, a typical weekday evening – the crucial fridge action occurs at 8 pm. That's when Man gets bored with the television (they specialise in watching

rubbish) and decides he's going to get one slice of cheese from the packet. 'I'm not having biscuits with it,' he announces to Lady, 'just the cheese.' He says this as if the absence of a single Jatz cracker turns the whole enterprise into some form of health camp.

At that moment, on an ordinary weekday evening, I charge up the hallway and skid to a stop next to Man's feet. I then sit, with my handsome head held high and tilted slightly to the side. This is a reprise of a performance piece I've been perfecting since I was a puppy, entitled *Best Dog in the World*. If I'm in position while he's still fiddling with the packet of cheese, he'll spot me and remove two slices of the dairy goodness, one for himself and one for me. He'll then serve it to me, in small pieces, while I sit next to him on the couch. It's hard for me to imagine that anything could be more delicious.

Well, it was hard to imagine right up to the moment of the Great Ham Incident.

Let me paint the picture. As you'd expect at a birthday party, there is food everywhere. I am being very restrained. No stealing from plates; no begging next to the barbecue. Just a dignified patrolling of the outskirts of the group, in line with my duties, and if someone offers a sliver of sausage, well, it would be rude to not to accept. But then they start putting away the leftovers. The fridge soon fills up, so Man says, 'Let's put the leg of ham in the

Esky. It's hardly been touched; we'll be able to live on it all next week.'

He takes out the leftover beers, throws away the melted ice, and lifts in the ham. He then goes out to the kitchen to get some ice packs to keep the Esky cold.

He's absent for around 40 seconds.

The Esky is on the floor in the laundry.

He has left the lid open.

The ham is sitting there, waving at me.

When he returns with the ice packs, he sees the ham. And he sees what has happened to the ham. The reaction is instant. 'Clancy! Where are you Clancy?'

By this time, I was out in the backyard, nonchalantly hanging out with some of my human friends. As Man approached the group, I decided to try out another of my performance pieces, this one entitled *Innocent Until Proven Guilty*.

At least the Great Ham Incident provided a focus for the next stage of the party. With Man's encouragement, all the guests crowded into the laundry. I rushed in as well, as I wanted to better understand the accusations I was facing. Once in the laundry, all the guests were invited by Man to examine one end of the ham bone, and the large bite that it had suffered. Man then said, 'Clancy, sit!' at which point he kneeled down and gently angled my head so that the outline of my jaw could be appreciated by the crowd.

'Witness the shape of the bite,' said Man, who appeared to be enjoying himself immensely, 'and witness the shape and size of Clancy's muzzle.'

It's true there was a striking resemblance between the two outlines – but, luckily, I had friends in the crowd.

'Circumstantial evidence only,' said one guest, Mick, a country solicitor and one of my favourite humans. 'No jury in Australia,' continued this distinguished legal gentleman, 'would convict on such paltry proof.'

'He was with us at the time,' said Claudia, also a personal favourite on account of both her kindness and her ground-breaking PhD on queer-film theory. 'Besides which,' Claudia observed, with her usual academic accuracy, 'he's such a handsome dog.'

'Are you sure it's not one of your drunk workmates?' said Jim, a neighbour whom I've always liked. 'Maybe an old journo friend just dropped to his knees and felt the need of a quick feed.'

At the time, Man bowed to the group pressure. The jury had voted 'Not guilty' and who was he to fight the crowd? And yet, ever since, he's been looking at me suspiciously. Five days have now passed without an 8 pm slice of cheese. How long will this continue? I cannot say, although I am working on a new performance piece, entitled *I'd Blame the Bloke Who Left a Leg of Ham Within Easy Reach of a Dog.*

By the way, on the advice of my friend Mick, the solicitor, I should perhaps mention that nothing contained in this letter will constitute an admission of guilt by the letter writer, or by any of his human supporters. This includes, but is not limited to, any admission of liability, wrongdoing or violation of law.

Thanks Mick!

Best from me.

Love,

Clancy

I'm aware that, occasionally, there are false accusations thrown up by the criminal justice system. I do not believe this is such a case. The forensics were compelling. The motive – ham! – was there. There was no real alibi. This is not Lindy Chamberlain, accused, tragically imprisoned, and yet finally exonerated. This is not France's Alfred Dreyfus, given a life sentence so undeserved that it was necessary to shout, 'J'Accuse!' at those who had conspired against him. This, surely, is not Socrates, that beloved philosopher, forced by the Athenian rabble to engineer his own death via hemlock, and yet still teaching as the life force slowly leached from his innocent and quivering body. Rather, we are dealing with a crowd favourite, a boulevardier with friends in the gallery, sidestepping all accusations with a wag of the tail and an appealing toothy grin. I don't hold it against him – I celebrate his popularity with my friends. And yet, I put it to you, a momentary slow-down on the cheese service was a perfectly reasonable response.

Age: **Three years and three months**

C/- Chateau Chaos

16 November

Dear Mum and Dad,

I wanted to reassure you about how well the training is going. It was slow when I first arrived – that's true – but things have improved. I now have my two humans almost fully under control. Repetition is the key. Hilariously, I've overheard the humans at the park saying, 'You need to do things 70 times before they understand.' They are talking about dogs, of course, but exactly that number of repetitions has, I've found, been highly effective in training both Man and Lady.

The toughest thing has been breakfast. It's my view that it should be served first thing. Dawn has sprung forth and is filling the world with its rosy hue. The birds twitter, the eyes blink open and suddenly the possibilities of the day lie spread out in all their enticing glory. A little sustenance, promptly served, matches the moment in a way I find defines perfection.

Yet, when I first arrived, both Man and Lady opposed this practical timetable. They had their own view of the correct ordering of events. It went like this:

6.30: Wake up, dawn spreading its rosy whatsits, followed by some groaning about the state of their knees.

6.32: Man offers tea to Lady. She accepts. It is brewed and served. I stand around, observing this activity, but find it boring. I don't take tea. I don't care for it.

6.40: The morning newspaper is fetched by Man from underneath the car – Man having to get down on his hands and knees in order to retrieve it.

6.45: Man delivers a somewhat tired comic monologue in which he jokes to Lady that the newsagent must be throwing

Training.

it there on purpose in a bid to increase Man's bending and stretching exercises. She pretends to laugh. God, that tea must be good.

6.50: Back in bed, one of them discovers a grammatical mistake in the newspaper's editorial, apparently 'a collective noun teamed with a plural pronoun'. This makes them both extraordinarily happy. Not for the first time do I wonder if the editor inserts intentional errors to supply pre-breakfast joy to middle-aged humans.

6.58: Filled with the contentment of those who consider themselves grammatically superior, Lady finally says, 'I might give Clancy his breakfast.'

Oh, God. Finally. I've been running around their bed for what seems like three hours. I've been looking at them with hungry eyes, doing my famous *Death Cannot be Far Away* pose. Some mornings, I consider filling in an organ donor card so they might better understand my perilous state.

Ignoring the looming emergency, Lady takes her time, carefully folding her newspaper in order to enjoy a later session of hunting down misplaced apostrophes. Finally, she gets out of bed. Finally, she gets my breakfast. Finally, she puts it in my bowl.

By now, it's 7.05. Why I have not passed out due to starvation remains a mystery. I inhale the food, in a process that takes some four or five seconds. It's delicious. Then again, it would have been delicious 35 minutes ago. I then nose about the empty bowl for another ten minutes, just in case I missed something in the first inhalation.

Why do I tell you all this? Because I decided to take the matter in hand. For the last 70 mornings, I have been trotting behind Man on his trip to the kitchen to make the tea. While he waits for the jug to boil, I've walked backwards and forwards between the fridge and my empty dish. It's been exhausting, arduous, frankly tedious work – all achieved on an empty stomach.

But I've pressed on. Every morning for 70 mornings. The aim: to create a link in his mind. Tea making. Fridge. Dish. Tea making. Fridge. Dish. Back and forth I go. Then, just last week, the breakthrough. He shouts up the hall, 'I might as well give Clancy his breakfast now, while I'm waiting for the jug to boil.'

Comes the response: 'Good idea. It might stop him making such a fuss.'

Well, hallelujah.

What's amazing is that, for the first 50 or 60 repetitions, you feel like you are getting nowhere. They give you that cute, quizzical look, turning their heads from side to side. They scratch their heads and say, 'What's wrong Clancy, what do you want?'

Then Eureka. Finally, they 'get it'. Even the slowest of humans is not beyond training.

And so Man serves my breakfast. Every morning since, he has repeated the action, bang on time. For him, deep in his subconscious, 'tea making' now equals fridge and then dish. It's automatic. He doesn't even know why he's doing it. Or who trained him.

I blame myself for not doing more in that first week or two after I moved in. Bad habits can become set in stone if you let them. I won't let it happen again.

Hope all is well in the country.

Love,
Clancy

I don't accept that I was trained in the way Clancy suggests. I simply decided, of my own free will, that it was more efficient if his breakfast was served while the kettle was boiling. Besides which, I was sick of the clackety-clack of his toenails walking backwards and forwards between the fridge and his bowl. He is, however, right about the newsagent. The man should be given a position on the Australian cricket team, such is his ability to reliably fling the paper to a spot from which retrieval each morning involves getting on your hands and knees, in a pair of shorty pyjamas, then wriggling your way forward, your bum facing the street. It's a mystery I haven't been arrested for offending public decency.

Age: **Three years and four months**

C/- Chateau Chaos

18 December

Dear Mum and Dad,

I hope things are going well for you, because they're somewhat difficult in the city. I hate to complain. You always told me that kelpies are a tail-wagging, head-tilting, up-for-anything kind of breed. All the same, it's Christmas time, and I don't think I can take much more of it. As you know, I share the house with Man and Lady, who are super-attentive, especially since I put the effort into training Man to serve my breakfast first thing, top priority, as soon as he gets up in the morning. He has so *completely* got the hang of it. Proud? Of course, I am. Effort in, results out. That message should go to young dogs everywhere.

But suddenly it's the festive season and both Man and Lady are totally unhinged. First there are the presents. Lady is obsessed with me, it's true, but she's even more obsessed with her two grown-up sons. They are very nice young men, don't get me wrong, but who else thinks that July is too early to buy them Christmas presents? Lady has the whole house stacked with gifts, but she now can't remember where she put them. She asked Man to bring the ladder, and they went through the high cupboards, in case she put them there. All they found was the present she bought when the older boy was ten not 30, a lost gift that's been sitting in a box beneath the bed ever since.

These days, that senior son is a chap with responsibilities. He has a partner. He has a house. He owns a small flock of backyard chickens, a station in life to which I myself aspire. Does he really want, all these years on, to receive a Nerf gun and a VHS of *The Nutty Professor*?

And where was the present she bought him for this approaching Christmas, the precise nature of which she cannot quite recall?

By this time Man was hyperventilating like a big fish hauled from the sea and thrown onto a jetty. He'd been up and down the ladder three times which, to hear his huffing and puffing, was the equivalent of an assault on Everest. 'Well, I don't know where you put the bloody thing,' he said to Lady, in a tone that didn't seem particularly festive.

I don't care for disputation. As a working dog, I have a practical impulse. Families, and I include myself as a member of this one, should operate as a united pack.

The next point of tension was the Christmas cards, which no

one had written, or even purchased, and already the first incoming card had arrived from overseas.

'But I thought no one sent Christmas cards anymore,' said Man, with a harrumph, as he turned the envelope over in his hand.

The card was from the Canadian couple with whom seasonal greetings had been exchanged for the past three decades, even though Man and Lady had long forgotten who they are. 'Are you sure you can't remember who they are?' Man said to Lady as he stomped up the front steps with their card in his hand. 'Your mother had a sister who moved to Canada. These people are probably connected somehow with your aunt, which means it's your responsibility to write back.'

Lady, who was searching the low cupboards for lost presents, straightened and turned to face him. 'Just because one person moves from England to Canada back in 1958, does not make their niece, yet to be born, responsible for all future communications between our family and the entire population of continental North America.'

Saying this, she glowered a little, which is not like her.

'Besides,' she said, 'you could just send back one of those Facebook Christmas card thingies.'

Man shook his head. 'I would send back a Facebook Christmas card thingy, but I don't know their surname. All it says here is

"Merry Christmas from Susan and Jack," and then an address in Alberta.'

Man and Lady looked at each other. They showed signs of having exhausted their pleasure in each other's company. To provide a circuit breaker, I decided to run around their feet, barking loudly.

Lady said, 'What's wrong, Clancy? Why are you making such a ridiculous fuss?'

Man said, 'It's Christmas. He's getting himself wound up like everyone else.'

Me? Wound up? I think of the human expression 'the pot calling the kettle black'.

Luckily, my intervention worked. They became so busy remonstrating with their rather clever dog – name of Clancy – they forgot all about poor Susan and Jack, huddled in their snow-pelted hut in Alberta, desperately waiting for some sort of response from sunny Australia.

For a moment, there was peace on earth. There was goodwill between Man and Lady.

Then, into the blissful quiet, Man asked a question. 'So, what would you like for Christmas, for yourself, as a present?'

At this Lady became wistful. 'I hoped you might have already thought of something …'

Man replied, with a giggle he mistook for charming, 'Well, not everyone buys their Christmas presents in July.'

My ears went up. My head cocked from side to side. It was like a radar dish, trying to process all available information. Rapidly, I reached a conclusion: a really quite dreadful argument was about to commence. I must act quickly.

I rushed in. I barked. I raced about. Just for the pure theatre of it, I upturned a water bowl.

Disrupting the narrative? Shifting the tone? Providing a fresh focus? Call it what you will, but it worked just as intended. By the time they cleaned up the puddle, they'd forgotten about Man and his attempt to justify his failure in the present department. Peace, once more, was restored.

I don't mean to brag, but I am the Christmas Dog.

Love,
Clancy

Are we that easily manipulated? I search for an answer. Oh, it seems we are. Mind you, it was just as well that Clancy stepped in, or the argument might have escalated. It's true that I don't enjoy buying presents. Christmas often seems to involve the purchase of something the recipient doesn't need, with money you don't have, resulting in a gift that is never used. Whatever happens, for instance, to all that overpriced soap? You can't open a bathroom drawer, anywhere in the country, without spotting a boxed set of soap, with a faux English name like 'Wodehouse and Baxter', 'Evelyn and Sebastian' or 'Fortnum and Harrod', and packaged in a frenzy of decorative ribbon. It's in the category 'too expensive to either use or to throw away' and so will sit there forever.

My best ever gift idea was to combine alcohol with classic literature, in matching sets. A copy of Tolstoy's short stories was matched with a miniature of Russian vodka; a book by Evelyn Waugh teamed with a small bottle of English gin; a copy of The Great Gatsby *presented with a flask of bourbon. Sometimes, I'd go all Aussie and team Thea Astley's* It's Raining in Mango *with a small flask of Bundy rum — both intoxicating; both proudly produced in Queensland. With this method, presents could be purchased for a whole squadron of friends and workmates in just two trips — one to the bookstore and one to the grog shop. Then, alas, the years roll by and you find yourself running out of classic novels and of friends who need more grog.*

And so you're back to soap.

At least Clancy is always easy to buy for. An extra-large bone, a toy that goes 'squeak' and a flash new collar. Perfect!

Age: **Three years and five months**

C/- Poste Restante

The Countryside

13 January

Dear Mum and Dad,

As you know, most of the time I live in the city, in a shallow and materialistic part of Sydney called Sydney. This letter, however, finds me in a major inland town called Goulburn. People are much nicer here. Earlier today, Lady went into the Goulburn supermarket while Man and I were left waiting in the car park. Here's the thing: I ended up feeling like a rock star. So many people came up for a chat.

'What's his name?' each person asked. Then, 'And how old is he?' After that, the compliments would start, with mention made of my two-tone muzzle, the markings above my eyes, and the alert way in which I tilt my head. One man, who at first seemed like a big gruff fellow, touched my forehead and then offered the observation: 'You can tell he is gentle just by looking into his eyes.'

If dogs could blush I'd have turned beetroot red.

Then other people arrived, and each person in turn dropped to their haunches and talked about their own dogs, and how I reminded them of Ranger or Molly or Scout. And then Man would ask questions about Ranger or Molly or Scout, and the passer-by would tell some heroic tale about their own dog, before giving me a final scratch behind the ears.

When it comes to a dog's ears, country people know exactly where to scratch.

One woman stayed for ages, explaining how her husband was a shearer. The husband had bought a dog to keep him company in the woolshed, but the dog only went to work once because the woman decided the woolshed was too hot and dirty. Not for the husband, but for the dog.

After that, she had the dog with her every second of the day, right up to the time the dog died, some fifteen years later, and she explained how that loyal, loving animal had made her feel safe whenever her husband was away shearing.

She grew pensive then bent down and gave me a long kiss on the forehead and told me I was 'a very good boy', which I accepted in the full acknowledgement that this tender kiss was meant for another.

By the time Lady came back, Man couldn't wait to list all the people he'd met, especially the shearer's wife. Then he smiled and said, 'People are so friendly around here. They kept coming up for a chat.'

No mention, you'll notice, of my role in proceedings. A dog, should Man not understand, is a well-known magnet for humans. A dog is a lightning rod for conversation. A dog, to coin a phrase, is the shortest distance between two people. Maybe Man already realises this. If not, he should try standing outside Woolworths Goulburn, alone, with his grey hair and thin lips, and see how many locals trouble him for his company.

Anyway, once the shopping was packed away, it was time to eat. We dropped into the service station on the edge of town. Man filled up the car, Lady ordered two hamburgers, and we sat at a small table in front of the petrol bowsers. Within seconds, an older couple, probably in their eighties or early nineties, approached, arm-in-arm, and both started talking simultaneously in the way that older couples do.

'Do you have a dog yourself?' Lady asked the pair, and the elderly folk answered as one, 'We have three dogs,' and then they listed the breeds and the ages, and some of their finer qualities, in a way that was a little hard to follow, as they were both giving the same information, in a slightly different order, at exactly the same time. But despite the stereo sound, they were lovely people, with many positive observations to offer in relation to both their own dogs and to yours truly. They wandered off, still arm in arm, like young lovers.

They were replaced by a kid, who came along and scratched my head, but didn't stop to talk, and then by the service-station man, who came and questioned me about whether I was thirsty in any way, and then brought me some water in a large metal bowl. Finally, the cook came out of the kitchen and talked to me as well. He didn't have a dog himself, not at that moment, but he really wanted one – a dog, he said, who would look precisely like me. 'A *dog* dog,' was how he put it, a phrase that I felt lacked a little in precision, even though I knew exactly what he meant.

Best bit of the story: this man, the young cook, brought out the hamburgers, then went back to the kitchen and returned, a little later, with a plate of chicken pieces that he'd cooked *especially for me*.

He said: 'I had to wait a while, because I had to let the chicken cool down,' as if he owed me an explanation for the delay.

Man and Lady said the hamburgers were the best they'd ever tasted. The same five-star review should certainly be issued in relation to the chicken pieces.

Tomorrow we go back to the city. I'm reluctant to leave. I find life in regional Australia rather suits me.

Love,
Clancy

Some may suspect Clancy of making up the stories contained in these letters. Did the cook really fry up some chicken pieces, especially for him? Was there really so many pats outside the supermarket, and so many compliments at the service station? Was there really a shearer's wife, like a character from a Henry Lawson story, talking about her loyal dog?

Since I was there, I can offer the assurance: it all happened just as Clancy describes.

Age: Three years and six months

C/- Chateau Chaos

20 February

Dear Mum and Dad,

Alas, I must break some bad news: things have taken a turn for the worse. The two people I live with, Lady and Man, have embarked on the most appalling new health and wellbeing regime. They start by lying on the floor, right there in the middle of the family room. As soon as they get down on their backs, I run over to examine them both. I give them a good sniff and nuzzle. I paw at their chests. I lick their faces. They are behaving so weirdly, I must make sure they are not dead. Then Lady responds as if I'm the one who is acting strangely. 'Shoosh, Clancy,' she says, 'the meditation tape is about to begin.'

I lie down next to them just to be companionable. The three of us are in a row – two humans on their backs, arms tucked in; me on my side, legs straight out.

Then the tape starts. You've got no idea the nonsense they listen to. It's a French woman, telling them to relax. Myself, I find it quite easy to relax. I don't even need to put on a tape! I just circle three times on the same spot, then collapse as if shot. 'Voilà!' (as the French lady might say): instant tranquillity.

It's tougher, it seems, for Man and Lady. They wriggle and scratch as they lie there. The French woman tells them to concentrate on each part of their body in turn. 'Focus on the top on your head,' she says. Then, 'Focus on your neck.' Talk about tedious. Personally, I tuned out the moment she said, 'Concentrate on your elbow.'

I don't even have an elbow.

The tape goes on for what seems like three weeks, with a lot of very unlikely material about 'breathing in the energy that is all around us', and 'basking in the love the universe feels for you'. Then Lady and Man, who used to be quite sensible, jumped up and stretched and went on with a lot of hooey about the positive energy of the universe. Next thing, they'll be wearing purple robes and I'll be eating kale for breakfast.

Speaking of breakfast, they are also on a savage diet. There's a lot of standing on the bathroom scales and moaning about how 'things went wrong in the run-up to Christmas', and how 'we let ourselves go', and 'it's time to do something'. I know what you are thinking: this sounds like a job for Clancy. If they are worried about eating too much, I'm perfectly placed to be of assistance.

And so, each dinner time, I position myself next to Man's dining chair. I don't roam or sniff or bark. I just sit there, head held high, a picture of self-control. From this position, I stare at each piece of food as he lifts it from his plate. My head swivels to follow his laden fork as it moves towards his mouth, and then swivels back to the plate as he skewers the next bit. By staring with such damp-eyed intensity, I hope to point out the obvious: 'That, my friend, is twenty calories right there. Eat it or don't eat it. It's entirely up to you. But – should you decide it's surplus to requirements – don't think it will be wasted. I'm willing to handle it. The calories don't worry me. The extra inches? No problem at all. If I need to spend another hour at the park, running it off, so be it. That's me. I'll just chase Pepper ten times instead of the usual eight. Me? I'm loyal to a fault.'

This gets me nowhere. He scoffs the lot. The French lady on the audio might go on and on about 'receiving and giving in a universe of love' but that doesn't seem to include sharing a bit of chook with Old Faithful.

Luckily, I do better with Lady. She ends up giving me a good chunk of her dinner. I go to bed that night feeling I've made a real contribution to her health regime.

That's the thing about dogs. On the TV news, they make such a fuss about the dog that barked and barked and thus woke up the family when the fire broke out; or the guard dog who repelled the thief by growling and snapping his teeth. Or consider the medals and awards that rain down upon the dogs who work with the police or in the army or helping the sight-impaired.

I'm not saying those dogs are not heroes. They are! They deserve the attention they receive. All I'm saying is that there are plenty of other dogs, less celebrated, who are doing their duty – unnoticed – in a steady, loyal way.

They do considerate things such as making sure their owners aren't dead when they are lying on the floor, having taken up meditation.

Considerate things such as scrutinising their owners' meals with a steady and unblinking gaze – thus highlighting that an alternative destination is available for each piece of food they may wish to avoid.

Considerate things such as refusing to leave the park when their owners first ask, thus ensuing extra exercise as the humans run around trying to catch their dog.

Would those humans like to thank us? They needn't worry. It's all part of the service.

In the meantime, roll on the end of February, when the French woman will go back in the cupboard, the diet book will be placed in the bin and Man and Lady will return to normal.

Until then,

Love,

Clancy

It's all very well for Clancy to criticise others, but – ahem – the scales at the local veterinary surgery do not lie. I notice, in his letters, he sometimes describes himself as 'twenty kilos of pure-bred Australian kelpie'. Yeah, sure. Who's running that dog's fact-check department. If he insists on watching me eat my food, I may start sitting by his bowl, watching him eat his.

Age: **Three years and seven months**

C/- Chateau Chaos

14 March

Dear Mum and Dad,

Yesterday in the park, an old fellow bent over and scratched me behind my right ear. So far, so good. The experience was quite pleasant. Then he turned to Man and said the most absurd thing: 'Dogs like to be scratched behind their ear because it's the only part of their body they can't reach.' What a load of bunkum. I scratch myself behind the ears all the time. Why would evolution, that marvellous system, have created a safe unscratchable haven for fleas, that natural enemy of the dog?

This notion about scratching is not the only piece of disinformation that circulates about dogs. Some people say we're colour blind, which also makes no sense. Show me a serve of chicken and then a serve of paprika chicken, and believe me I can pick the difference, using sight as well as smell. (I prefer the non-paprika chicken. I say, let the main ingredient sing!)

Why do humans invent this sort of rubbish about dogs? It's not as if we make up stories about human incapacity. You don't find me saying, 'Oh, apparently Man can't reach his own bum.' Or 'When a human scratches themselves it means they have fleas.' Or 'You can't teach people anything new once they get past about 43.'

Humans would be wise not to turn this into a competition, especially since dogs are, in nearly every aspect of life, superior to people.

People, for example, are always singing their own praises when it comes to technology. They say, 'We're so clever we can invent anything. We invented the internet. And we invented Wi-Fi.' Fair enough, but if they are so good at high-tech, why can't they develop a machine, deployable at airport security, that can detect the presence of illegal drugs, gunpowder or – here's the Australian preoccupation – fruit?

Answer: they can't; otherwise they would.

Instead, the whole edifice of the Australian Border Force is piled on the shoulders of one overworked beagle called Terry. Terry can instantly pick out an ISIS bomber, an ice-dealing member of the Triad, or a bloke with a pineapple up his clacker, all while hardly breaking his stride. If you could patent that dog's nose you'd be richer than Bill Gates.

Same thing with medical science. Science has spent billions on cancer detection systems, and yet – in recent experiments – they have resorted to training dogs to sniff out cancers. These canines are saving lives as surely as if they had jumped into a freezing river and swum a rope to a drowning child. One study has revealed that the medical dogs get it right with an accuracy of about 97 per cent – hardly surprising when you consider our sense of smell is rated as 10,000 times better than that of humans. In fact, some experts offer this analogy from the world of sight: if humans can see half a kilometre away, a dog can see nearly 5000 kilometres. Even further if the thing we're examining is a bowl of chicken.

It's not just the nose that's superior when it comes to dogs. The ears are pretty good as well. They can hear higher frequency sounds, as well as distant sounds. One expert says dogs can hear sounds four times further away than can be heard by humans. It's why I rush around when a thunderstorm is approaching, while Man dithers around saying, 'What's wrong, Clancy? Has something spooked you?' Five minutes later, the penny drops and it's a case of 'Oh, I get it. It's a thunderstorm.' By which time, of course, I've grabbed the safe spot under the bed. Too late, old boy, you'll have to find your own hidey-hole.

Humans and dogs share 84 per cent of their DNA, which is surprising when you think of how different we are. Obviously, dogs dedicate our unique sixteen per cent to important skills in the area of smelling, hearing and loyalty. The question is what are the humans doing with their unique sixteen per cent? Presumably, there's a chromosome or two for getting stressed over how they look (we dogs never bother with looking in mirrors), a chromosome for doing their tax (even rich dogs let others handle their financial affairs), and probably whole sections of the brain dedicated to getting upset over things they can't control (a human speciality, it always seems to me).

Are there activities in which a dog is less adept than a human? Of course. We are unable to pick up dog hair, despite shedding it each day. We're unable to operate anything but the simplest washing machine. In terms of literature, we often wait for the movie.

The point is, we can do most things that are worth doing. And that includes scratching behind our own ears.

Give yourself a scratch from me.

Love,
Clancy

I'm happy to accept that dogs are clever, but the picture Clancy paints of his super-intelligent species is not the whole story. A case in point: the other morning I finished off a jumbo tub of yoghurt and gave the empty container to Clancy, thinking he might like to chase it around the backyard and lick out any remaining yoghurty goodness. He did a mighty fine job. The team from CSI Miami would have been unable to locate a single cell of remaining yoghurt in that container.

However, large quantities of yoghurt remained on Clancy's forehead, where it stayed for much of the day. If, when reading these letters, you tire of Clancy's superior tone, do allow a picture to form of a dog's head decorated with dairy.

And while we are on the subject of dog intelligence, I have recently met a dog who is scared of his own farts. He hears a loud noise from behind and spins around in surprise and consternation. He'll then pause before repeating the sequence: fart, surprise, then walking around in circles in a vain investigation of the cause. He is left tormented and angry, and yet unaware he is the author of his own distress.

Humans are not smart all the time, I grant you that. But neither are dogs.

Age: Three years and eight months

C/- Chateau Chaos
19 April

Dear Mum and Dad,

The most hideous thing has happened. According to the people I live with, I urgently required a bath. I can't believe how rude they were about it. 'Clancy, you need a wash,' said Man, having already filled up the washing tub with water. What am I? A piece of laundry? There was no inquiry as to whether I'd like a wash. There was no 'I say, old boy, perhaps a bit of a splash of the old acqua minerale might be quite pleasant.' Instead, in an instant, he'd taken off my collar and I felt myself being lifted skywards. There was no time to state my objections which, as it happens, were backed by RECENT SCIENTIFIC RESEARCH.

I was wriggling my body from side to side to indicate that Man might like to pause, put me down and retire to the kitchen to examine that morning's newspapers, for if he did so he would surely come across this COMPELLING NEW STUDY. To be specific, work conducted by Professor Andreas Gutzeit, of

Switzerland's Hirslanden Clinic, which found men's beards carry far more germs than a dog's fur.

According to the study, only recently completed, 'The researchers found a significantly higher bacterial load in specimens taken from the men's beards compared with the dogs' fur.' I enjoyed the story so much, I read it three times.

The Swiss research came as no surprise to me. Personally, I'm fastidious about cleanliness, which is why I spend every spare moment licking my paws, scratching my tummy, rolling in freshly mown grass and shaking my body. I'm a relentless self-cleaning machine. Certainly, when I come back from the park, I always vigorously shake myself as soon as I'm in the front door, sending any dirt or grass fragments flying. It's a full-body shake, which starts at my nose and gets more intense as it runs towards my tail. Imagine Beyoncé dancing while being engulfed in an earthquake.

As Man lifted me towards the tub, I performed the same dynamic movement, just to remind him of the unnecessary nature of this whole enterprise. My thought process was, 'By the time I get in the tub, there won't be a speck of dust on me, so WHY ARE WE BOTHERING?' He seemed oblivious.

He lowered me towards the water, my legs windmilling like Wile E. Coyote going off a cliff. Luckily my limbs found purchase. I had my front paws on one end of the tub, my back paws on the other, my body locked rigid. I'd decided I wasn't going anywhere. This did not go down well. 'Clancy,' said Man, 'stop being ridiculous. It's just a bit of a wash. You don't want to be all germy and dirty.'

Sure. Fine. But if he's so worried about cleanliness, shouldn't he focus elsewhere? For example, on bearded men.

Occasionally, Man and Lady have visitors and they sometimes include gentlemen with beards, beards which are often excessive in volume. I watch as these men come up the steps and enter the home. Never have I seen a single bearded gentleman give himself a good shake before he comes through the door. Some of them also have very hairy arms, and – I also notice – never do they pause to give themselves a good lick.

A bearded man makes a particularly poor dining companion, at least as far as a dog is concerned. With normal, clean-shaven humans, the odd crumb will fall from their lips to the floor, thence to be rapidly consumed by any observant hound. With the bearded man, there's nothing. They are operating a large crumb-catcher, perfectly positioned below their mouths. You can sit at the feet of a bearded man from one end of dinner to the other and not get a morsel. He probably takes the lot home, secreted in his face fuzz, ready to feed a family of four.

These were the ideas I was trying to communicate as my body was lifted over the tub, but, alas, my arguments were ignored.

The metal ledges on the side of the tub were slippery and Man seemed to have quite considerable experience in the dark arts of dog washing. I took a moment to commiserate with my dear departed forebear, Man's first dog, Darcy, on whom these devious techniques had clearly been perfected.

Suddenly, Man deftly prodded my back legs one way, and my front legs the other, detaching me from the tub's edge, and I was in the drink, my whole body submerged in this ghastly warm water, Man squirting dog shampoo at me, disgusting perfumed stuff, all the while telling me, 'Good boy, Clancy, what a tremendous dog you are Clancy.'

Look, frankly, it was not so bad.

I just wonder, next time, for the sake of human health, could he pick a more deserving target, leaving me to my own cleaning regime, while he instead pops over the road to visit that bearded bloke in number 53.

'Fancy a bit of a scrub,' Man might say to Gary, proffering a bucket and a brush. I'm sure the recipient would be no less resistant than myself.

Until next time,

Love from Clancy, your (temporarily)

wet and bedraggled puppy

I notice that, in his letter home, Clancy makes no mention of the period that led up to the forced washing. He doesn't, for example, reveal our trip that day to a friend's dairy farm, and his own decision to roll in grass that was strewn with cow pats. Or the way he ducked into a muddy dam for a quick refresher. Or his celebratory trip to a very large pile of fertiliser, stored in the dairy shed ready for spreading. That dog needed a wash. I was doing him a favour. As the old advertising campaign expressed it: 'Don't wait to be told …'

Age: **Three years and nine months**

C/- Chateau Chaos

24 May

Dear Mum and Dad,

Here in the city, there's been the most regrettable outbreak of madness at the local dog park. There are two pugs with whom I am well acquainted. It's true they've been putting on a little weight, but nothing prepared me for the horror I encountered this morning. Both dogs were wearing identical brightly coloured coats, covering the whole trunk of their bodies, from neck to tail. I say they were brightly coloured, but that doesn't quite capture it. The coats were a rich purple, like a bishop's cassock, with large letters picked out in hot pink. The letters filled the entire body of both the dogs, on both sides, in the manner of a mobile billboard.

The letters read: 'Do Not Feed Me'.

Oh, the indignity! Oh, the public humiliation! It's true the pugs were running around happily – 'waddling' may be the more accurate word – but I'm sure they were both hurting inside. They were being fat-shamed in a most reprehensible way.

Once again, humans bring to the dog community attitudes which they would not apply to themselves. There are, for instance, many humans of my acquaintance who might benefit from a warning sign printed on their clothing, advertising their personal failings. I know Lady would quite like to see Man, especially on a Saturday night, wearing a fleecy top emblazoned with the slogan 'Further Supply of Beer is Not Required'. Or 'Has Already Eaten a Whole Pack of Cashews'.

Everyone has failings, I acknowledge that fact. Those of us in the dog community are not perfect. I, for one, could take a little more time to eat my dinner. 'Chew, savour, then swallow,' is what I instruct myself as I approach the bowl, but then – half-a-second later – I notice the plate is already empty. The speed with which the food has been hoovered up is baffling, even to the dog that's done the hoovering. That's why I always stay there for a few minutes, working at the empty bowl in the belief that further food may present itself. It never does.

A personal failing? Yes. But don't put it on a coat – 'Bolts His Food' – and make me wander around in public. Who are these people? Small-town judges from Texas?

I've been known to dig, that's true, but only as a means to economic independence. And – okay, confession time – I have a deep mistrust of distant thunder. Again, does that mean I should wear a jacket with the humiliating commentary 'Suffers From Irrational Fears'?

What about a bit of dignity for the dog world?

It's not only the slogans emblazoned on the coats. It's also the names that humans give to their dogs. How would you like to be called Winnie the Poodle, Mary Puppins or Muttley Crue? Again, the indignity! And what about the pretentious names like Wittgenstein, Tolstoy or Schopenhauer – designed so the human can yell, 'Come here, Schopenhauer,' and everyone in the park will know they once read a book?

Here's another question (and yes, I've become a bit political since I turned three): since when was it right to allow your two-year-old child to supply a name to a dog – a sophisticated animal which, for that moment at least, has an IQ far superior to the child? The result: a dignified and unique creature going through life responding to the name Woof. Or Wag. Or Doggy. Cute when you're a puppy. Less cute when you're a senior dog with responsibilities. Why can't we have proper names, like Steve or Bronwyn? Or ones with a real flavour of Australia. Clancy, for instance, is an excellent name.

It's all part of the critical gaze one is subjected to as a dog. All the popular tropes are about food snaffling, crotch sniffing and leg humping, instead of a more noble narrative in which we guard the tribe, lower your blood pressure and bring constant joy. Merely patting a dog for fifteen minutes can lower blood pressure by ten per cent. Owning a dog, in one recent study, was associated with a 3.34 mmHg decrease in systolic blood pressure. Yet all we get are a lot of jokes about how lazy or daft we are.

George Carlin: *'What do dogs do on their day off? Can't lie around – that's their job!'*

Merrill Markoe: *'I sometimes look into the face of my dog Stan and see a wistful sadness and existential angst, when all he is actually doing is slowly scanning the ceiling for flies.'*

Dave Barry: *'Dogs feel very strongly that they should always go with you in the car, in case the need should arise for them to bark violently at nothing, right in your ear.'*

Well, ha ha. Very amusing. Make it about anyone other than a dog and you'd be up in front of the anti-discrimination commission.

It's not as if humans are perfect. For every dog who steals food from the table or chews a favourite shoe, there's a human who eats with his mouth open. Or, worse, breaks wind and then blames the dog. Put him in a T-shirt that says, 'I Blame Others for My Farting' and see how he likes it.

Imagine, for example, a railway station at peak hour with all the humans lined up, waiting for the train to arrive. What would happen if all the humans had to advertise their imperfections?

Cast your eye along the waiting crowd. 'I'm a Workplace Bully'; 'I Eat Too Much'; 'I'm Self-involved'; 'All I Care About is the Number of Likes I Receive on Instagram'.

Those slightly overweight pugs? They are starting to look pretty good.

In the end, we'd be better keeping these things to ourselves – each of us, dog and human, privately working on our faults – without the harsh glare of public blaming and shaming. For me, that means slowing down when eating my dinner. For Man, it means foregoing that last beer. And for the pugs it may mean choosing to say no to that proffered treat.

What's good for the goose is good for the gander. In other words, what applies to the humans should apply to my pals, those two little pugs.

Hope all is well in the country.

Love,

Clancy

I don't like Clancy's tone when it comes to the frailties of his human companions. As it happens, I'm already on a diet, with no need for a warning printed on my fleecy top. In my case, the diet is the '5:2' regime promoted by Dr Michael Mosley, in which you restrict your eating for two days a week, then eat normally for the other five. I believe it's having an impact, although not everyone agrees. When I last took my shirt off, my friend Matt looked at me and inquired, 'Have you considered the 4:3?'

So, to be fair, maybe Clancy does have a point.

Age: **Three years and ten months**

C/- The Ashram
Via Chateau Chaos
2 July

Dear Mum and Dad,

It's your dog Clancy, writing with the news that I've become a Buddhist. Well, I think I've become a Buddhist. All the talk around here is of 'mindfulness', which is apparently a Buddhist practice. When Lady and Man take me to the park, they are full of it. Mindfulness I mean. 'We should stop and look at this tree,' Lady says, and they both stand there looking at this tree. It's so boring I'm forced to break their reverie by weeing on the thing.

Later, at the café, Lady says to Man, 'After you've had your coffee, you should just sit there and think about the coffee-ness of the coffee you've just had.' It was at this point I realised, I've been practising mindfulness all along. After I have my dinner – admittedly chicken, so not fully Buddhist – I always contemplate the chicken-ness of the chicken I've just had.

Here's my 'practice'. First, I eat the chicken, normally in one dramatic inhalation so I can get onto the mindfulness bit. Second,

I lick the empty bowl for some minutes, round and round and round again, dislodging quantities of dinner that are practically homeopathic. Third, I stare at the empty bowl for up to ten minutes, contemplating the universe and what it might bring. (More dinner would be a good start.)

After eating their own dinner, Man and Lady throw themselves on the couch. They make a sound that could be mistaken for 'Om' but actually sounds like 'Aaargh'. They whinge about how tired they are, before turning on a television program of, frankly, disappointing quality. They are in no way mindful in their actions. Meanwhile, lying on the floor in front of the couch, I attempt to demonstrate a method of 'mindful' sitting, circling three times in my customary manner before collapsing suddenly in a pleasure-seeking heap, thus embracing the world of stillness and contemplation. Yet, despite my easy-to-follow example, not once do I see Man and Lady circling a chair before plumping down on it.

The next day, we head off in the car to visit friends, but Man is anxious he won't remember everyone's name. 'So, what are the children called?' he says, drumming his fingers on the wheel.

Lady sighs. 'The girl is called Rebecca and the boy is called Troy.'

'Sure, that's right,' says Man, as if he knew all the time. 'And the girl is, like, ten years old and the boy is maybe twelve.'

Zen Therapist

Replies Lady, 'The girl is now 22 and studying law, and the boy is 25 and married with two kids. His children are named Elise and Rachel.'

The car descends into bickering, but what do I care? The back window is slightly open and I have my nose pressed to the gap. I let their words drone on in the background as I lose myself in the scents of Victoria Road. Ah, the French bakery on the right. Next, the Irish pub on the left. We're about to cross the Gladesville Bridge, and as we hit the rise of the bridge, my nose fills with the smell of water, that whole system of bays, beaches and tributaries. It's intoxicating. The Harbour, I've always thought, is Sydney's front yard.

Lady, meanwhile, is listing the occupations of all the people who will be at lunch, with Man repeating the information as if he were a five-year-old reciting his times tables. 'So, he's in IT and she's a doctor, and the neighbours are called Karen and Ewan and they own a hairdressing wholesale business,' he says, repeating the sequence a few times.

Really, why do they care? At the dog park, I make friends with twenty dogs a day. Only with my closest friends, do I even bother learning their names. Sure, I know Pepper and Lucky, Archie and Watto, but that big brown dog who dribbles a lot and loves being chased? Don't know, don't care. Couldn't even tell you the breed. We just get down to a few invigorating rounds of Chasey Chasey.

After about an hour of driving, we arrive at our destination and head into the backyard. I'm trying not to listen, but I can still hear Man showing off his newly acquired knowledge: 'How's the legal profession going, Rebecca? And the kids? Are they well, Troy? And Karen and Ewan, the hairdressing business, how's it travelling?'

He's committed to getting all the names out in one rush, before he forgets them, even though there's no space for anyone to answer. It's 'mindful' but only in the sense that it briefly employs what little is left of his mind.

Meanwhile, I spot two little kids. I'm guessing their names are Elise and Rachel, but really does it matter? I roll on the grass, the sunlight on my tummy, and wriggle my legs in the air. The little girls tickle me and scratch behind my ears. I don't mean to brag, but they consider me an excellent example of all that a dog can be. The three of us are completely, and blissfully, living in the moment.

Life in town has its annoyances but also plenty of joys. As a Buddhist, I choose to concentrate on these.

Bye for now.

Ommm.

Love,
Clancy

It's true that Clancy treats his food bowl in a special way. He calls that way mindfulness. I call it magical thinking. The food goes into the bowl and it's instantly gone. He then stares at the empty bowl as if he had nothing to do with the food's disappearance. He could have savoured each piece, judging its provenance and flavour, before selecting a second morsel. But instead it's a vacuum extraction. Then he commences the period of hopeful waiting. Forget Buddhism; it's more like a cargo cult. If he stares at the bowl hard enough, he's assuming additional supplies will drop from the sky.

I don't mean to be too critical. I go through a similar process at about 9.15 on a Friday night, convinced that I cannot have drunk all the beers, and that there must be one lurking in the fridge, perhaps hidden behind a cauliflower. Sometimes I'll move the cauliflower three times, just to make sure. My experienced tip for Clancy: I am always disappointed.

Generally, though, he is right about his own ability to live in the moment. One day I'm going to get on my back, lift my arms and legs as he does, and wriggle in the sunlight. It looks so much fun. I just wonder who might be willing to scratch my tummy.

Age: **Three years and eleven months**

C/- Clancy's Personal Training and Walking Service
Chateau Chaos
1 August

Dear Mum and Dad,

I have news of a business idea, which I'm now eagerly developing. It started with a casual comment made by Lady as we headed off on our morning walk. 'Just imagine,' Lady said to Man, 'if we didn't have Clancy. We'd hardly get any exercise. He's the one who makes us walk.'

I couldn't agree more. Every morning, I'm required to virtually carry them out of the house.

'Just let me finish the newspaper,' one of them will say. Or, from the other, 'I haven't had my cup of tea.' Or even, 'It's a bit cold this morning, maybe we should just stay at home.'

I leap around. I whine at the door. I point to the park with my nose. I sit on the newspaper to make it clear that the economics correspondent has delighted us with his musings for long enough. Finally, it works. They stumble out of bed and drape themselves in various ill-fitting garments. I, meanwhile, am ready to go: dressed in my own fur, offset with a green collar. We leave the house. This after forty minutes of assiduous encouragement from yours truly.

Once we arrive at the park, I notice a personal trainer at work. He's dressed in a black Lycra track suit. A group of people are standing in front of him, all looking half-asleep and reluctant. The trainer's job is to encourage these individuals to exercise. 'Come along,' he shouts. 'You can do it. Get on with it.'

They sigh and whinge, but eventually do what he says. It's no different to what I do every morning, and yet – here's the shocking bit – he gets paid to do it. That guy is onto a neat scam. In the light of such profiteering, how fair is my situation? I now realise that I've been fully employed for the last four years as 'personal trainer' to Man and Lady. I supervise all their exercise. I give them all their motivation. I won't hear the word 'no' even when it's raining. And yet where's the financial compensation?

According to my research, personal trainers charge up to $40 a person. That's $80 for Man and Lady. Often, we attend the park twice a day. You don't have to be a mathematical genius to do the sums. I should be on an annual income of $58,400, instead of which I get the odd handful of kibble and a serve of raw chicken. Tell that to the Fair Work Commission.

Pay me properly and I'd be quite happy to make my own arrangements when it comes to food. It would be organic chicken for a start. Plus the grain-free kibble – the expensive one that promotes a shiny coat. If there was any leftover money, I would buy my own couch, ending the arguments over whether I'm allowed to make myself at home on theirs.

There's also no reason why I couldn't help other couples. There's a period in the middle of the day when, frankly, I'm under-employed. There's a bit of hole-digging to get on with, but I'd be willing to leave that until the weekend. That's why I'm thinking of getting some flyers printed up. 'Dog Walking Service' seems to cover it, as it's a service in which a dog takes you walking. I'd include the quote from Lady as a sort of testimonial: 'Clancy is the one who makes us walk.'

And, of course, it's not just the exercise. I'm also providing a social introduction service. Left to their own devices, Man and Lady would just be sitting at home, friendless sad sacks, quite pathetic really. Instead, we're out in the park. I chase another dog, the dog chases me, and hey presto, all the humans get to meet and are soon talking and laughing.

My speciality: I make sure to only chase dogs whose humans will, I believe, prove interesting to my clients, Man and Lady. For instance, Pepper's owners, Lady and Lady. Working together, Pep and I get everyone laughing which, frankly, is what these humans need.

A dog, it strikes me, is an anti-aging cure – a source of vitality, exercise and human interaction. My services should be prescribed by the local GP. Allocate me a Medicare provider number and I'd be willing to bulk bill. And, of course, it's not only me. When I go to the park, I can see all the dogs are providing exactly this service.

Sometimes, they go above and beyond. One thoughtful hound, worried his human has performed insufficient 'steps', can be seen leading her on a chase around the park, the lady giving her lungs a workout by screaming, 'Come! Come!' By this clever means, the women's exercise time is extended until – in the view of her trainer – a full aerobic workout has been completed.

Another, rightfully, is concerned about her owner's upper-body strength, and is requiring a stick to be thrown 20, 30, no 40 times, just so her owner's right-arm muscle is given a proper work out. A third has 'stolen' a bag of treats – successfully causing all the humans in the park to run after her, this way and that, until all of them are panting for breath. That Lycra-clad personal trainer, still bellowing at his customers, dreams of achieving such excellent results.

Should we dogs be thanked? Yes, but more to the point, how about a regular cash transfer to one's account?

Hope all's well in the country. I shall report back once my new business is up and running.

With all my love,
Clancy

Clancy, it must be said, is a very good judge of people. It can't be chance that he only ever plays with dogs who turn out to have taken some pleasant people for a walk. I'm now in the position that half the people I know are those I first met at the dog park. Some people might believe this strange. 'Oh, how did you find your accountant?' a friend might ask. 'Oh, I met her at the dog park.' Then they crinkle their nose, as if this is the world's most peculiar place to find an accountant. Why? What would be a better place? The local greengrocers? A ten-pin bowling alley?

I also have a wonderful painting by an up-and-coming artist. ('Oh, how did you meet him?' 'At the dog park.') And I have even enjoyed a special beauty treatment with Nick, or as I know him, 'the owner of Mirabelle and Bentley'. My skin, since you ask, looked fabulous for weeks. So please don't think I'm odd for preferencing people to whom I've been introduced by my dog. At least I know they are wise enough to appreciate Clancy.

Age: Four years

C/- Chateau Chaos

13 August

Dear Mum and Dad,

Celebrations have been raging here for my birthday. I'm turning four, which seems an excellent age, although according to Man and Lady, this must be multiplied by seven in order to ascertain my age in human years. I've always thought this system was total rubbish and yet they persist.

When I was one year old, they told me I was seven in human years. At the time, I knew some human seven-year-olds. They were pleasant enough, but entirely unfocused. Give them a mob of sheep to round up and they'd have lost interest after five minutes. They'd have been slumped at the edge of the paddock, playing Minecraft on their laptops, while I'd be left to do all the work, leaping and twirling with aplomb.

Then, when I turned two, they once more multiplied by seven and told me I was fourteen years old. Suddenly it was all, 'Ah, Clancy, you are a real teenager now.' Teenager? What? Was I mooning around writing bad poetry? Was I standing in front of the mirror pushing my fur one way, then the other, before sighing heavily? Was I suddenly talking endlessly about Margaret Attwood, Jack Kerouac, Fyodor Dostoyevsky and other authors I'd never read?

Not guilty, your honour. Yet I'm labelled a teenager.

Name me the fourteen-year-old whom you'd allow to mind the house, as I am required to do all the time. Or the fourteen-year-old who'd be more than happy to fetch his own dinner, just leave the ingredients within easy reach. Or the fourteen-year-old willing to sit there, giving companionship for hours on end while Man or Lady watch *The Masked Singer*, an 'entertainment' so unsuitable for dogs that my IQ drops 10 points between each ad break.

And on all those nights I've been left alone in the house, guess how many wild parties I've held at the last minute, teenager-style, inviting 93 'close friends' via WhatsApp, leading to the arrival of 415 not-so-close friends who will variously throw up on the front steps, break the toilet seat and steal the sound system?

Give me a moment to count. That's right: zero.

Next up, I was turning three, and there was much talk of a '21st party'. Suddenly the 'multiply-by-seven' system seemed to have its advantages. I'd heard a description of a recent 21st birthday party and started daydreaming of what my own might involve. It would probably be like Lucy's: a 1970s disco-theme party with everyone dressed up in wigs and spangly tops while 'Stayin' Alive' blasted out on the dance-floor. I guessed there'd be a good spread, just as Lucy and her friends had enjoyed, with lots to eat and drink, and then some terrific speeches. In particular, Man would deliver the humorous tale of how I'd once chewed his favourite boots, but that's all forgotten now, and what a fine chap I've turned out to be, and really they scored in the lottery of life when they got me, and how about we all sing a rousing chorus of 'For He's a Jolly Good Dog'?

But, breaking news, the big day arrives. No party, no friends, no speeches. Just one dried pig's trotter, a tickle under the chin and a new soft toy.

Speaking of which, what's with the soft toys? Another one arrived this week, to mark my fourth birthday or, as they seem to think, my 28-year-old celebration. It's a weird looking monkey that squeaks loudly when you bite it, a feature that is a fair distance from entertaining. Certainly, my attempts to play with it in the backyard have failed to augment my popularity with the neighbours.

As it happens, 28 is the same age as Man and Lady's younger son, who, for *his* birthday, was given a cheese-making kit, a new doona and some live chickens for his backyard. I could have used all of those, especially the chickens. It hardly seems fair, this disparity in presents – a point I made, with some elegance, by digging a hole and burying the squeaking monkey. Man appeared annoyed by the large earthworks in the middle of the back lawn, but I spotted a look of gratitude from the couple next door.

How long will this 'multiply-by-seven' system continue? When I'm eight, I'll be close in human years to Man, which frankly leaves me a little depressed. Will I really be like him – making strange noises when moving from a prone to upright position? Will my interest in human society be suddenly focused on the proposed changes to the superannuation system? Will I suddenly be found at home on a Saturday night calculating whether one should watch a 'long show' on the TV or a 'short one', given that it's already 9.45 pm and we'll all need to go to bed soon?

Spare me. Still, there are advantages. By age nine, I'll be 63 and eligible for a seniors card, providing all sorts of discounts. The only catch: you have to work less than twenty hours a week to qualify, so I'll have to cut back on work at The Diggings.

And by fifteen, I'll be 105 in their system, at which point they might finally treat me with a bit more respect. My biggest question: should I expect a telegram from the Queen?

Anyway, hope all is well in the country.

Love,
Clancy

Clancy only knows about the Seniors Card because of our friend Neil, who is delighted with his. As soon as Neil received it, he rushed around and showed it to both Clancy and me. Using this card, he pointed out, you could catch the train all the way from Sydney to Gosford for just $2.50.

'Yes,' I said to him, 'that's fine, but what if I don't want to go to Gosford?'

'Go anyway,' Neil said, 'and just contemplate how much money you are saving. You can then spend the money you've saved at the cinema, and if you use the seniors card when you are there, you save another $2.50, which will then cover another trip to Gosford.'

He stood, beaming at me and Clancy, admiring his own mathematical skills. 'It's a virtuous circle in which everything pays for everything else.'

What I didn't realise was that Clancy was listening to every word. God knows what other insane ideas he's picked up from listening to Neil.

Age: **Four years and one month**

C/- Chateau Chaos

17 September

Dear Mum and Dad,

Some say dogs are not musical, but I've recently taken up singing. It's something that's been forced on me by the tedium of our nightly regime. After dinner, Man and Lady just sit there on the couch. They might read a book. They might watch TV. But nothing more interesting. Once the clock has gone past 9 pm, there's a prohibition on all the things that give life its spark.

There is no walking, there is no running, there is no preparation or consumption of food. There are no trips in the car. There is no sweeping of the back porch. The lawn mower, a device which always provides excitement and intrigue, is never employed. If I were to suggest any of these activities might be embraced in order to break up the ennui, I would be told, 'Don't be daft, Clancy – it's night-time.'

So, there we are, like clockwork, Man and Lady, sitting on the couch, occasionally chatting. It's like being stuck in a play by Chekhov.

Even worse, there's nothing to distract me from my rumbling belly. By 9 pm, I haven't eaten anything for … well, I can't recall when I last had some sustenance. It was probably weeks ago. There is a real possibility I will die of hunger in the long hours between now and morning. It's urgent that I secure some titbit to tide me over. But how to get their attention? How to warn them of the crisis that's impending? There's no alarm to ring. No glass box with 'Break in Case of Emergency'. Only one thing, in my experience, works. And that's a rendition of what has become known as 'Clancy's Cheese Song'.

I sit at the feet of Lady, with my front paws tidily arranged, head held high, looking up at her with pleading eyes. It's a theatrical pose I call *Faithful to the End*. The eyes, of course, are a little moist. I'm emotional, as you might expect of a dog who is contemplating his own imminent death from starvation. I tilt my head to one side to signal the start of the performance, and then launch into the chorus of 'Clancy's Cheese Song'.

'Oh, oh, oh,' I sing, and then – reaching for a few higher notes – 'Oh, oh, oh.' The song is quite melodic. There are a couple of verses – they go 'Oh, oh, oh,' then 'Oh, oh, oh,' – and then a final chorus of 'Oh, oh, oh.' A perfect composition? I don't like to say, but it's certainly an advance on 'Clancy the Flying Dog', that clanging ditty oft sung by Man.

The good news is that the song works like magic.

'He's singing his Cheese Song', says Lady in a tone of admiration, as if I were the world's one and only singing dog. (There are actually plenty at the park.) Then she turns to Man, 'Oh, do get him a slice of cheese.'

Suddenly, the gloom lifts; the Chekhov play is over. Pushing himself off the couch, Man goes to the fridge. He opens the door and a heavenly light bathes his face. He reaches in and removes the Tasty Cheese Slices packet. The lid pops open with a sound that reminds me of the singing of angels. It is the sound that cheese would make if cheese could sing.

He hands the slice to Lady, so that she might tear it into little pieces, as that's the way I like it. He then announces that he 'might as well have a beer, since I'm up anyway,' then Lady says, 'Actually, while you're up, could I have some strawberries and yogurt with maybe some slivered almonds on top?' And Man says, 'Oh, I might have those as well. They are delicious.'

Pretty soon, he fires up the sound system and sips on his beer, while Lady feeds me the tiny pieces of cheese, each of which I take from her hand in a very dainty manner, and then they both dance around with me, everyone laughing and happy. At one point, they even play a song by Little Richard, the lyrics of which go 'A-wop-bop-a-loo-bop-a-wop-bam-boom,' which makes me think that this Little Richard hails from a similar song-writing tradition to my own.

Anyway, that's the story of a dog who has been – literally – forced to sing for his supper.

Should I complain to the RSPCA? Not really. If anything, it's proof of the transformative power of just one song, if delivered with sufficient panache. An evening rescued from boredom! A dog saved from certain death! A small shot in the arm for Australia's brewing and dairy sectors!

Think what I could achieve if I composed a few more tunes.

I might start working on it.

Love,

Clancy

Did I read that right? He takes the cheese 'from her hand in a very dainty manner'? When there's cheese to be had, you could lose a hand to that dog.

Age: Four years and four months

C/- The Diggings
Crumbling Manor
13 December

Dear Mum and Dad,

Another letter from the city and – as always – a fresh horror to report. This week the household has acquired a robotic vacuum cleaner. The infernal device has been making my life hell ever since it arrived. Whenever I fall into a blissful slumber, I hear it starting up in the next room. It seems to know the exact moment I'm enjoying a moment's repose. As you can imagine, I go *insane*. I rush into the room in which the succubus is doing its evil work, barking to warn others of the danger in our midst. I circle around the hateful object, snapping and growling. My hair goes up on my back and neck, so that it might be aware of the threat I represent. As it moves towards me, I leap over it, in way that would signal dominance to any normal sentient creature.

Amazingly, *disrespectfully*, it takes no notice. It continues to whizz away in its insolent and yet totally useless manner. It heads towards one side of the room, then bounces into the wall like a

GRRRRRR

VRRRRRR

ROBO-VAC

Natural Enemy

drunken idiot. 'Sorry, mate,' it seems to say to the wall, before turning around, and then – oh amazing – managing to pick up a single bit of dust.

Big deal. What a huge nothing.

I make my contempt clear via some more barking, at which point Man looms up at the back door. I'm not saying that Man is putting on weight, but he does tend to block out the sun at such moments. He completes his progress into the room and, unbelievably, it's me that's in the firing line.

'Why are you making such a commotion? It's only the new vacuum cleaner. Just because it's robotic and internet-connected, there's no need to panic. It's just the modern world finally arriving at Crumbling Manor.'

First point, Crumbling Manor is my joke. Check out my previous letters home – I've been using jokes like this for years. Second point, for God's sake, spare me the sanctimonious tone. While it's true that Man is quite adept when it comes to scratching my head, he is a total ignoramus when it comes to technology. The idea that he's giving me advice on 'accepting our digital future' is frankly ludicrous.

This is a chap who hardly knows how to watch television. To catch the 7 pm news he has to start at 6.30, such are the complexities of him getting off Netflix or Stan and onto the normal stations. I see him at work with the remote control, his tongue stuck out in concentration. Dogs are meant to admire their owners, but this particular *tableau* does not help. True fact: when Lady is out, and thus not available to operate the set, we hardly watch TV at all. 'Just as easy not to bother,' Man says to me, as he settles down with a two-day old newspaper, thus denying me the chance to bark angrily at *Q&A*, which happens to be one of my favourite activities.

Another thing about Man and technology: he can hardly cook a meal without complaining about the control panel on the oven. 'There's too much choice,' he says to either Lady or me, whoever is in a mood patient enough to listen. 'Why don't they just have an ON switch and then a dial to choose the temperature?'

Of course, as nearly everyone knows, there are reasons for those extra settings. For example, people might have a hungry dog and need to defrost a little extra chicken.

Admittedly, I'm a digital native. I was born only four years ago. Netflix is five times my age; Amazon a lot older. Digital skills come naturally to me. An example? Right now, when I'm home alone, I am experimenting with Alexa, seeing what that particular device can do for my quality of life. It's voice activated and I have a voice. Typical of her efficient ways, Lady has already loaded her credit card details, along with various default settings. If I time things right, three barks in the correct sequence could result in the delivery of four pizzas and a side order of garlic bread. At the moment, I'm holding back from placing this order, but only due to uncertainty as to how to provide a tip for the delivery person.

Generosity, after all, is my byword.

Except, of course, when it comes to the vacuum cleaner. I mean, really what's the point? If Man had to push around the Dyson once a week, would it really be a disaster? Might a bit of physical exercise – I don't want to be too personal here – be a positive for the old chap rather than a negative? Maybe, if I timed it right, I could ask Alexa to list the robotic vacuum cleaner on Gumtree – free to a bad home – and instead order some gym equipment.

That's the thing about technology. As a digital dog, it's a matter of picking and choosing. Some of it's great. And some of it's just an annoyance.

Love from me,
Clancy

It's not true what he says about the television. I've been practising and can now turn the thing on in as little as five minutes. As for the oven, it really is impossibly complicated. There's a drop-down menu which you can only read by getting down on your hands and knees and peering at it through a pair of spectacles. Do you want fan bake, grill or pyrolytic cleaning? Would you like to scroll down to a particular type of food – say roast chicken – enter the weight of the bird and then allow the machine to choose the cooking method? This option really is on offer. The only problem, by the time you decipher the controls, the heat from the oven has fogged up your glasses to the extent that you can no longer see anything.

In order to cook a chook, you'd be faster lighting a 1920s Aga with wood-shavings and a flint.

Age: **Four years and five months**

C/- Chateau Chaos

15 January

Dear Mum and Dad,

Why is life in the city so perplexing? For example, the most common game in the local park could be called 'Watch as I Throw Away Your Stuff'. Here's how it works. The human gets their hands on some treasured item – a ball is the most obvious example – and the dog begs for it to be given back. The dog looks up, cocks his or her head in an appealing manner, and makes a noise, easily translatable as: 'If you wouldn't mind, terribly, could you please give me back my ball?'

Instead of acceding to this very reasonable request, the human instead throws the object as far away as possible. The dog then runs off, fetches the ball and returns to the group. The dog looks at the human and tries to convey the thought: 'I know you strangely threw away my ball for no good reason, but I managed to save the situation. No need to apologise. I'll just lie here and cradle it between my paws to keep it safe from some future calamity.'

It's at this point that the human leans down, grabs the ball from the dog ... and throws it away once more.

Some days, I feel like calling the RSPCA.

If we wanted you to throw the ball, why would we so strenuously refuse to give it up? Why would we sink our teeth into the ball, shaking our heads from side to side, as the human tries to wrench it from our jaws, giving ourselves whiplash in an effort to maintain possession? Think about it, people. I know some dogs want you to throw the ball, but – in most cases – they're the ones who will happily hand it over.

Even weirder, how come most dogs agree to fetch the item once it is thrown, sometimes retrieving it some 20 or 30 times in a row? Don't the dogs realise: every time they fetch the ball, it reinforces this rather inappropriate human behaviour? It's as if these dogs are completely unaware of the basic principles of animal training.

What would happen if we dogs handed out the same treatment to the humans? If we started routinely throwing away their favourite stuff? I could take Man's wine catalogue and throw it down the back of the garden. When he says, 'Where's my wine catalogue?' I could indicate the back door with a wave of my muzzle. The unspoken sentiment: 'Go fetch, sport – you could do with the exercise'. What's good for the dog, one might contend, is good for the owner.

Some humans, admittedly, throw the ball high into the air, which at least allows a modicum of sporting prowess in its capture and return. There's a dog I know who seems to have an urge to fly, so enthusiastically does he launch himself into the air, intercepting the ball as it rises. He leaps skywards, the body at first stretching out, front paws reaching upwards, at which point the jaws clamp onto the ball, and the torso forms a compressed curve, ready for the descent, the whole elegant tableau of flying dog and captured ball then gliding back to earth. It's some combination of Australian rules and an aerobatic stunt display. Put it on at the MCG and you could sell tickets.

Far too often, though, 'Watch as I Throw Away Your Stuff' involves nothing so theatrical. It's just a desultory kicking of the ball. The human takes a giant swing with their leg, hits the ball at an oblique angle and the thing piddles to a stop in the middle distance. It's hardly Tim Cahill in action. Many dogs, quite correctly, treat these mullygrubbers with the contempt they deserve. The humans are left to stomp off and retrieve the ball themselves. This at least gives some innocent amusement to those of us in the cheap seats.

But for most dogs there's no respite from the Sisyphean task: ball thrown, ball returned, ball thrown again. What's worse, many of the humans now use a sort of hand-held trebuchet – flicking

Eternal Mystery

the ball on a low trajectory from one side of the park to the other. For the dog: maximum effort, minimum fun.

Why do so many dogs, each morning, participate in this tiresome ritual? My theory: they are trying to trick their humans into at least a little activity – a kick of the leg, an unflexing of the arm, the occasional short hike when they might themselves pick up the ball. The humans in the city are loaded down with problems – physical, psychological, attitudinal. Many are quite fat. We so-called 'companion animals' do our best to help them get moving, even if it means putting up with this constant attempt to throw away our most treasured stuff.

In the city, every dog is a therapy dog. That's what I've discovered. We must do our best to rise to the occasion.

All the same, could someone come up with a better game?

Love,
Clancy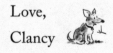

Clancy, it's true, has no interest in chasing balls. If you throw one, he just looks at you as if to say, 'You threw it; you go pick it up.' He's not the only dog to have this attitude. One puppy I know got so sick of chasing the ball, he grabbed the thing, dug a hole and buried it. When I heard that story, I thought of the way the sports master forced me to play ball games at school. I told him I was reluctant, but he refused to listen. If only I'd thought of grabbing the football, digging a hole and burying the bastard, I might have had a happier childhood.

None of this means that Clancy is not interested in physical activities. He plays particular games with particular dogs. With Archie, for instance, the game seems to be called 'Who Can Put the Other Dog's Whole Head in Their Mouth?' The game looks alarming to outsiders but is much enjoyed by both participants. Neither Archie nor Clancy play this game with any other dog. Georgie, another favourite down at the park, goes into a frenzy whenever she sees Clancy. She's a tiny thing, but she darts up towards his mouth, licking it again and again, like one those suckerfish that clean the teeth of sharks. According to her owners, it's only Clancy that inspires this frenzy of practical dentistry.

Weird? Definitely. Then again, Clancy is handsome.

Age: **Four years and six months**

C/- Chateau Chaos

16 February

Dear Mum and Dad,

As you know, I've recently become an activist for dogs' rights – pointing out the indignities that are heaped upon those of us in the canine world by certain humans. Here's a fresh example: people have a bad night's sleep and then blame it on their dogs.

Down at the park, you hear it all the time.

'How are you, Janet?'

'Oh, terrible. I didn't get a wink of sleep, due to this tiny fellow.'

They'll then point out their dog, a perfectly harmless little fluffy, describing how the animal spent the night prowling around, growling randomly, and then jumping in and out of their bed.

Then they'll say: 'I just wish he'd learn to sleep properly.'

By this time, listening into the conversation, my fur is bristling. No one is asking the obvious question: what was the disturbance that caused the poor dog to wake up in the first place? My bet is the disturbance was human.

In our house, Man is the worst sleeper imaginable. I'm in my own bed, blissfully snoozing, when he and Lady turn out the light. She is off to sleep in a moment, but not him. With him, it's all twisting and turning. Then he starts groaning and sighing. This – as I suppose is the idea – causes Lady to wake. She says, 'Why are you moving around so much?' and he says, 'I can't get comfortable. I don't know where to put my arms.'

And she says, 'Well just don't put them anywhere near me.'

She then goes back to sleep, leaving me to the monitor the situation.

By now he's facing the alarm clock, which is always a mistake, as he starts calculating the time before the alarm will go off. This involves him mumbling aloud as he does the subtractions and additions, and then moaning when he realises he's heading for less than six hours' sleep. I hear him turn over, adjusting the pillow so he gets the cool side, then rearranging his arms. That's when Lady wakes up again. At this point she's annoyed. She says, 'Your hand is touching my hair. It feels like spiders are crawling in my hair. Please put your hand somewhere else.'

This causes him to sigh, and then he flip sides once more, which means he's facing the alarm clock again, and so he starts counting off the hours, by which process he works out that another 30 minutes have gone, meaning he's down to five and half hours' sleep. He then mutters as if he's the most put-upon human in the whole wide world.

It's at this juncture, and only at this juncture, I decide to cut my losses and get out of my own bed. According to sleep scientists, if you can't sleep it's better to walk around and do some other activity, rather than build up a psychological association between your place of sleep and an habitual state of sleeplessness. I get up quietly, as I don't want to disturb Lady, and proceed down the hallway with a light clip-clop-clip-clop-clip-clop of my nails. This, luckily enough, means I'm well placed to hear that some people are walking up and down in the street outside. Their precise identity is unclear, but it's obvious they are up to no good. I assume they are casing the joint, preparatory to staging a violent break-and-enter. I decide to let off a volley of loud barks and alarming growls, snapping my teeth at the front door, and willing my voice to be as deep and threatening as possible. The good news is that it works. The robbers immediately move further up the road – presumably to number 67, a home guarded by an asleep-at-the-wheel Labradoodle called Trixie who, halfway through the home invasion, may well attempt to lick them to death.

That's when Man – despite all my good work – decides to remonstrate with me. 'Clancy, can you please be quiet? Can't you see I'm trying to sleep? Will you stop making such a racket.'

I know. Another example of Pot. Kettle. Black.

And yet, the immediate threat having passed, I decide to

humour him. I get back into my kennel, curl up on my mattress, and start daydreaming about my future career as a police dog. I'd fight crime in the inner city, assisted by a very appreciative handler, probably a smart young policewoman, and be awarded with a feature on the TV news and the occasional medal.

This pleasant fantasy is soon interrupted by Man, who climbs out of bed, announcing that he needs to have a wee, which is frankly more information than I could possibly require. He returns, shifts around for a while, and then actually falls asleep.

Bliss. Short-lived. He then starts snoring at a volume which may well loosen the tiles in the back bathroom. I beckon sleep, but sleep never comes. How could it? The noise is incredible. I'm surprised the local council doesn't show up with a decibel monitor.

So, think of me. And of all the other dogs. Here's our fate: to endure a night filled with human snoring, human disputation and even an attempted human home invasion. Then – next morning, at the dog park – to be told that, in every home, the problem just happens to lie with the household's faithful hound. It's a human racket. In more ways than one.

Anyway, please spare a thought for all the dogs who could do with a little more sleep, including one called Clancy.

Love from me.

I think it's fabulous that Clancy has become such a campaigner on dog issues. I do wonder, however, whether this is the right issue for him to choose? His description of saving the household from certain attack makes for very exciting reading – but was he right in his suspicions? While it's true that the hour was late, he responds in exactly this manner at every hour of the day and night. The street outside might be listed as a public thoroughfare, but its use by an actual member of the public appears to be an indignity up with which he will not put.

As to his main complaint: it's true that I sometimes have trouble sleeping and can't quite work out where to put all my arms. It's a curiosity of being human, that – as you approach the bed – you appear to have two arms, hanging meekly from your sides, but once you get into the bed, they multiply until you resemble some sort of Hindu god. You can slip one arm under the pillow and fling another over your head, but there always seems to be one or two left over. I remember once hearing about the International Space Station, and how astronauts sleep – floating above the bed to which they are tethered, zero gravity supporting their every limb. No wonder people dream of a career with NASA.

If I were Clancy, I'd just be grateful I'm a dog, with two front paws, two back legs, and the ability to form into a ball when ready for sleep.

Age: **Four years and seven months**

C/- Chateau Chaos

15 March

Dear Mum and Dad,

It's your dog Clancy, writing from the city. Quick question: when did I leave home? My memory: when I was about ten weeks old. Have I prospered since then? I think I have. Have I troubled you in any way, requesting your assistance? The answer, I believe, is in the negative.

What a contrast with the world of humans. Man and Lady have two sons, nice young chaps. Both of them lived at home all through their teenage years. By then they were able to eat solid food, run around and keep themselves clean, yet despite these achievements, they were still living at home – aged fifteen, sixteen and even seventeen – like dependent puppies. Why?

Even now they have left, Man and Lady are at their beck and call. As soon as one of them rings, it's like the Situation Room at the White House. Incoming! All hands on deck! Quick – the offspring need us!

The other day, it was earth removal. One son wants to dig out some concrete from his backyard. Fair call. Speaking for myself, I love digging. But how was he planning to get rid of the rubble? It was a case of Man to the rescue. Following a phone call, we go around, the two of us. The young prince has extracted a mountain of concrete pieces and is hoping that Man might shovel the pieces into a series of wheelbarrow loads and them take them away in his ute.

Here's my observation. Man will do anything to please his son. He throws himself into the task, shovelling then wheelbarrowing then shovelling again, the sweat pouring off him, and all the time saying, 'Don't worry, son, I've got it, it's not heavy at all.' Through all of this, the poor old bloke has turned puce and looks like he's about to have a heart attack. His earth-moving days are surely over, or at least they should be.

Don't get me wrong, I admire Man. But this is pathetic. If his son said, 'Hey Dad, I like the look of your shirt,' he'd take it off on the spot and hand it over. Luckily, it's now so sweaty and dirt-stained the son is unlikely to ask.

We drive away, the ute groaning under the weight of the concrete, which Man then has to shovel out of the tray once we get to the tip. The tipping fee, I happen to notice, is $63, a sum of money which – give me a moment to do the arithmetic – could result in the purchase of 7.6 kilos of raw chicken pieces, if chicken were to be prioritised over concrete removal.

Meanwhile, Lady has heard that the other son might be coming up for the weekend. By the time we arrive back at home, it's as if preparations were underway for a Papal visit. The spare bedroom is being aired, doona covers are being washed, and a number of cookbooks have been left open on the kitchen table. As soon as we enter the hallway – me sprightly, Man hobbling after all the shovelling – Lady starts peppering us with questions.

'Do you think,' she coos, 'that he'd like the chicken schnitzel, which was his favourite when he was fourteen, or the Sri Lankan fish curry, which was his favourite when he was seventeen? Or maybe the home-made lasagne I used to make when he came home from university?' She's also been through all the old DVDs, selecting out the favourite movies from his childhood, just in case he has the sudden urge to watch *Raiders of the Lost Ark*, or *Ferris Bueller's Day Off*.

I know sibling rivalry is supposed to be between brothers of the same species, but occasionally I do feel its sting. I'm the one still living in the house. I'm the one who gets Man and Lady out of bed. I'm the one who sees that they are properly walked each morning. And yet none of this fuss is for me. Imagine, for example, the scale of The Diggings if I had access to Man's ute.

A few days later, excitement mounts with the now imminent arrival of the first-born son. It's Odysseus returning to Ithaca.

It's Aragorn once more entering the kingdom of Gondor. It's the triumphal march from *Aida*. The young fellow arrives and Man is instantly outside, offering to carry his bags and suggesting he move the ute from the driveway so the Crown Prince might park his own car in the shade.

That night, both the boys are present for dinner, and the bounty knows no end. The fridge is full of craft beer, carefully selected, and every fruit bowl is overflowing. It is Arcadia. It's the Garden of Eden. It's the Horn of Plenty.

Yours truly? Well, I sit between both sons and am rewarded by them tickling my ear, stroking my neck and making regular observations about my fine qualities as a dog. Oh, and both boys, when Man and Lady are distracted, slip me some chicken.

They appear to be competent and kindly young men, the legacy, perhaps, of a childhood that went on for longer than appears strictly necessary. So, maybe it turned out for the best. Who can be sure? I merely note that some members of the household have achieved a state of decent adulthood without the lengthy preparation that appears necessary for young humans.

Hope all is well on the farm.

Love,

Clancy

Clancy does have a point. Why does it take young humans a period of 20 or 30 years to leave home, when most species manage it in the space of weeks? Even worse – Clancy doesn't mention this – the departing offspring then leave all their stuff behind. At our place, there are boxes of it, pretty much everywhere.

Here's the problem. We're sentimental about the childhood stuff and cannot throw it out. The teddy bears, the Lego castles, the complete history – presented in photocopied sheets – of the Leichhardt Saints Under 11 soccer team and its heroic third-division triumph over the Burwood Titans. No way can any of that stuff be thrown out.

The offspring, meanwhile, are sentimental about the detritus of late adolescence. The Farewell to Year 12 memorial T-shirt on which obscene messages have been written by their school chums. The arsenal of slightly busted Nerf guns. The nylon onesie outfit which one or other of them wore in order to wow friends at a fancy dress party. No way, in their view, can any of that stuff be thrown out.

Put it all together – then multiply by any number of children – and there's no room left in the house. We live like mice, scampering around the piles of boxes, bags and plastic crates. Which at least gives Clancy something to play with.

Age: **Four years and eight months**

C/– Chateau Chaos

13 April

Dear Mum and Dad,

My career as an advocate for the rights of dogs continues apace. I've been collecting examples of the unconscious bias against dogs contained in many human expressions. When learning to use a keyboard, for instance, people practise by typing a phrase that uses all the letters of the alphabet – 'the quick brown fox jumps over the lazy dog'.

Why is the fox heroized in this way, despite being a vicious yellow-eyed predator, while the loyal dog is rendered as some sort of bludger, asleep in the corner?

What is the evidence for this much-repeated calumny? Why can't the 'quick brown dog' jump over the 'lazy fox'? It's prejudice, plain and simple. As is the phrase 'Let sleeping dogs lie', a particularly tedious repetition of the slander that dogs spend half their time asleep.

Equally objectionable is the expression 'a dog's breakfast', implying a total mess, a situation without order or logic. Really?

Personally, I despatch my food in one inhalation. In the unlikely event that a single piece of kibble escapes the bowl, I delicately and immediately consume it. Where is this dog who leaves their breakfast lying around in a mess? I'm yet to meet them.

The cause of such linguistic bias is quite mysterious, at least to me. Most humans say they are pro-dog. They appreciate our constancy, our friendship, our desire to please. They recognise the value of our work with those who live with a disability; they understand our role in bio-security, sniffing out illegal imports; they cheer on our ability to sit among a group of humans and, at the very least, look as if we are interested in the conversation.

But where is this reflected in the language?

Okay there are a few positive phrases. 'Man's best friend' is accurate, as is 'dogged' for the ability to keep at a task longer than can reasonably be expected. I'm a strong supporter of the phrase 'works like a dog', as it reflects our indomitable spirit, even when working conditions are difficult. And I don't even mind 'the tail wagging the dog', as I have, on occasion, wagged my own tail with such vigour that my whole body has swung from side to side.

But consider the prejudice that's also on offer. A person who dobs on another is 'a dog', as if a real dog has ever informed on someone. And a bad film is 'a dog', whether or not an actual dog is involved. Indeed: the phrase 'It's a dog' was recently used to describe a film called *Cats*, an invocation of our name in circumstances which seem particularly hurtful.

'A dog-eat-dog world', meanwhile, is used to describe the human ability to shunt aside all morality when there's profit or advantage to be had. Talk about upside-down logic! Humans are the ones driven by self-interest. A dog, nearly always, is driven by loyalty and love. I suggest a new phrase – 'It's a human-eat-human world' – used to describe those rare moments in which a dog acts with selfish intent.

Is there any human failing for which a dog is not made responsible? A human breaks wind and it's 'the dog did it'. A human drinks too much alcohol and then requires 'a hair of the dog that bit me', as if their current state of listless incapacity was the result of some sort of canine attack, and not their own sad lack of self-control. A human keeps bad company, and, as usual, we're back to blaming dogs: 'If you lie down with dogs, you get up with fleas', as if a passing infestation of fleas is the equivalent of signing up with the Mafia.

An even sharper example is the child who fails to complete a school assignment. What do they tell their teacher? That's right: 'A dog ate my homework'. This barefaced lie fails even on the grounds of creating a good alibi. There's no detail; that's the giveaway. What's the name of the dog? What breed? If the story were true, wouldn't you say, 'Our family dog, name of Harry, ate my homework'? The term 'a dog' implies the homework room is full of roaming strays whose precise identity is unclear, a situation which seems unlikely.

Another dubious scenario is that a human, having finished eating dinner in a fancy restaurant, will think of nothing other than the needs of their dog. 'Could I have the leftovers in a doggy bag?' they'll ask the waiter, and the waiter – perhaps themselves a dog lover – will hop to and hand over a container of delicious food.

Here's the bitter truth: WE NEVER GET THE FOOD. The greedy humans scoff the lot. Often in the taxi home. In fact, most humans who ask for a doggy bag DON'T EVEN HAVE A DOG!!!

Finally, the humans throw a bit of ageism into the mix, using the phrase 'You can't teach an old dog new tricks'. What rubbish. I, myself, am proof that's not true. I'm four and a half years old and I've learned how to decipher, parse and utilise human language, all in the hope of pointing out prejudice wherever I see it.

My conclusion: I see a lot of it.

I hope you'll give me your support, for the sake of dogs everywhere.

Love,

Your loyal dog, Clancy

Clancy's argument is hard to fault. Why do we say, 'sick as a dog', when they are so very rarely sick, at least compared with humans? Perhaps we need some new more realistic sayings. For example, 'Barking up the correct tree', since mostly there really is something sitting in the branches. Or 'sick as a human'. Or 'A sleeping dog is just a dog waiting for something to do'.

From this human at least, it's full support for Clancy's latest campaign.

Age: **Four years, nine months and a bit**

C/- Chateau Chaos

20 April

Dear Mum and Dad,

It's your dog Clancy here, writing from self-isolation in the city. Like you, I'm sure, we're currently affected by the coronavirus lockdown. Frankly, it's not that great being bunkered down in 'iso'. Man and Lady are surviving on food from the pantry, which has led to a diet of chickpeas, sardines and baked beans. Their self-isolation, in other words, is necessary for more reasons than the coronavirus.

There are other negatives. Those languid times I used to so relish – there in the middle of the day, when they were otherwise occupied – are now ruined. Normally, left to my own devices, I'd settle down and watch an Attenborough documentary. Or put in some work on The Diggings. Maybe rip a cushion to shreds.

No longer. They have control of the TV set and are insisting on completing a new program of daily exercises 'designed for the young at heart'. This means attempting to touch their toes while being bellowed at by a young man from Essex. Personally, I don't understand the appeal.

After this, they lie on their backs and 'meditate'. This means we're back listening to the French lady who tells them to 'breathe in the goodness of the universe'. Yeah, the universe right now is chock-a-block with 'goodness'. I'm pretty sure the virus has seized control of their brains.

While they're lying down with their eyes closed, I hold back for a while, allowing them to nod off, and then – quite suddenly – I give both their faces a big wet kiss. There's nothing that can achieve 'a sense of being alive in the present moment' than a dog licking your face when you are least expecting it.

But what do I get for my troubles? 'Oh, Clancy, leave us alone. Can't you see we're meditating?'

Actually, I decide to give the meditation a go, lying there on my side, my legs stretched out, while the French lady instructs 'Scan your body for signs of stress.' This leads me to focus on my stomach which, as usual, is suffering the stress of being scandalously empty. I'd certainly like to 'breathe in the goodness of the universe', especially if manifested in the form of chicken.

There are plenty of pieces of the aforementioned in the freezer – I saw Man bag up a fortnight's worth of Clancy rations at the beginning of the week – but how much longer before their own supplies run out and they start raiding my stuff? I won't be impressed if they nick my chook, especially as I had attempted to encourage proper preparation. For years, I've been agitating for my own chicken run, up by the back fence, as well as for a small flock of sheep, operating under my daily management. In the past, these ideas were greeted with laughter, as if I were a country bumpkin not up with city ways, but suddenly they are looking rather prescient.

Another thing that's looking smart is my attitude to home security. Even before the lockdown, I would always bark when any group of more than two people walked past our house. For years, my policy was met with scorn. 'Oh, Clancy, stop it. That's just a few kids heading down to the park.' Well, mate, check in with the police commissioner and I think you'll find he's come around to my way of thinking. Now I'm in line with official advice.

We're still going down to the park, of course – the humans standing in a loose circle, shouting salutations to each other while the dogs play. The trips, however, are not quite as frequent as they once were, so we've also taken to 'having drinks' over Skype with my friend Pepper and her owners, Lady and Lady.

Both couples fetch their drinks and their peanuts, while Pep and I are given nothing. Some party!

Even worse, halfway through the conviviality, Man picks me up – twenty kilograms of pure-bred Australian kelpie – and holds me in front of the camera, my legs dangling in mid-air, my paws trying to find purchase. Talk about undignified. He treats me like a sack of potatoes. Then he angles my head towards the screen, which is not an action I had required him to take.

'There you are, Clancy,' Man says. 'There's your friend Pepper.'

Well, sure on the screen I can see a dog that looks a bit like Pepper – there's a cute face surrounded by black-and-white hair that stands on end as if she'd been recently electrocuted. But, here's the point: there's nothing to smell. If they want the digital world to work for dogs, they've left out the main thing. The smell. What's the point of me and Pepper getting together if we are both denied use of our noses?

What's Pepper been up to? What's the food that's been served up at her place? Has she met any other dogs? Frankly, I don't know. It's like humans having a party in which no one is allowed to speak. If this is the so-called 'digital future', I don't care for it. Sometimes, I think the IT people are not at all attuned to the needs of dogs.

Anyway, like all things, we have to make the best of it, spending time with those we care about the most. And, with luck, Man and

Lady's chickpea supplies will run out and the air in here will start to clear.

I haven't lost my joie de vivre and I hope you haven't either.

Love,
Clancy

Clancy may think self-isolation is difficult for dogs, but I think it's worse for the humans. You end up with too much time on your hands. At our place, first to suffer were the books.

Let me paint the scene. I start dusting them, just to fill in a little time, but soon find myself organising them. I pull all the books off the shelves and stack them on my bedroom floor. But what system should I use to rearrange them? Alphabetical would be too easy, given the amount of time I am trying to use up. So instead I choose a north–south system, whereby they are organised first by continent, and thence according to latitude. The books on the top shelf will, under this method, come from further north than the books on the bottom shelf, which, to me, is only sensible. If an author is from, say, Crete, you'll find their work in the European section in the sunny climes down on the lowest shelf.

It's the perfect activity for lockdown, as it requires extensive research every time you attempt to replace a single volume. Is Tolstoy closer to the north pole, or does victory go to that beaten-up paperback from Stieg Larsson? *Throw in* Miss Smilla's Feeling for Snow *and, within minutes, I am sitting on my bedroom floor, surrounded by books, and entirely stumped by my lack of geographical knowledge.*

Clancy, meanwhile, enjoys the fact I'm suddenly on his level and therefore available to be nuzzled.

To judge the latitude issue properly I need to ascertain where each writer died – in this case, the Astapovo Railway Station for Tolstoy, Stockholm for Larsson, and, well Peter Høeg's not yet dead, but I decide to mark him down as Copenhagen and if he changes his mind could he please drop me an email?

Then I look up the latitudes – 53.2098 N for Tolstoy, 59.3345 N for Larsson and 55.6761 N for Høeg – and so, after a good ten minutes' research, I'm in a position to place the Larsson on the top shelf, with the Høeg to its right, and then finally the Tolstoy. I now have three books on the shelf, with a further 400 stacked around the room at my feet. At this point I give up, fearful of the impact of this task on my mood and on Clancy's patience.

Instead, the dog and I will tackle the filing cabinet.

First to go are the bank statements which, as I read them, send me into a funk of despair after I realise how many years it's been since the bank paid me a cent of interest. I seethe with rage. I then uncover a file of car insurance papers which – following fifteen minutes' work with a calculator - prove that if I'd 'self-insured' back in 1983, and then just banked the money each year, I'd now be driving a Maserati. I also uncover three retailer's gift cards, all past their expiry date. By now I have the contents of the filing cabinet all over my bedroom floor, fighting for space with the books. Clancy is barking at me, as he might a thief. Certainly, the room now looks as if there's been a violent break-in.

I decide the whole 'bedroom tidy-up thing' is too depressing to continue, so I regroup in the kitchen where I will rearrange the herbs and spices, which have long been in a mess.

I take out every packet and jar from various drawers and pile them on the kitchen table. As with the books, I need to first establish a method for organising. I could divide them into 'commonly used and 'rarely used', or into 'India' and 'Mexico', but that would require too many closely debated decisions and I don't want to involve Lady, as she is restacking the DVDs according to the funding model used for their production.

I decide to go alphabetical with the herbs and spices, by which process I discover that almost all of them begin with the letter 'c', which requires me to sort unto the second letter, and thence unto the third and fourth letters – caraway, cardamom, cayenne – which leaves me constantly chanting the alphabet like a six-year-old. Really, it may be easier to just leave them splayed all over the kitchen table in various *random piles. That way Lady can sort them out when she's finished with the DVDs.*

Clancy has stopped barking but is now looking at me with his head tilted to one side, eyes questioning. In the lexicon of Clancy expressions, this one means: 'Do I ring Triple Zero now, or do I wait another ten minutes?'

Clancy decides to wait.

Alas, having abandoned three tasks, I am still at a loose end. This is when my eye alights on a box in the laundry cupboard marked – in large Texta letters – STUFF WORTH KEEPING. It's a box that I haven't opened in twenty years.

Oh, boy. I fetch it down. First thing I find is an envelope full of old keys, marked 'Old keys, unclear what they are for'. I then pull out an envelope full of envelopes, all with dried out seals, marked 'Envelopes, various sizes'. And then a parcel full of pencils which need sharpening, marked 'Pencils which need sharpening'. I'm almost expecting a jar called 'Pieces of string too short to use'. It's the most useless box of stuff ever collected and makes me wonder what the miserable tightwad fool who inscribed this box as STUFF WORTH KEEPING was thinking, using handwriting which is so clearly mine.

With Clancy attentively watching, I tip everything from the box onto the floor, filling the one square of floorboards not already littered with books or discarded files. And that's when I find them, right at the bottom of the box. There are two envelopes marked 'Tooth from Tooth Fairy' – each containing a tiny tooth, one each from our now grown-up sons. I open the envelopes in turn, allowing each tiny tooth to tumble into my hand. I find myself transported to another time and to another place. This is just as well, because someone has turned this spot into a total tip.

And, for once, it isn't Clancy.

Age: **Four years and nine months**

C/- Chateau Chaos

20 May

Dear Mum and Dad,

I've spent much of the evening under the bed, where I have been the subject of mocking comments from both Man and Lady. 'It's just a thunderstorm,' they say. 'Why are you being such a scaredy cat?' What? I beg your pardon? I'm being called a *cat*, just because I take precautions during a period of lightning strikes? Lightning strikes are dangerous. Don't take my word for it. Look it up. There are no statistics recorded for the way they injure dogs – which is typical – but nearly 25,000 humans die each year. More than 200,000 are hurt. Common injuries include broken bones, confusion, hearing loss, seizures, burns and ocular cataracts. If I were Man and Lady, I'd forget the ridicule and the snide cat references and petition me for a little extra space beneath the bed.

Why are human beings so anxious about some dangers and yet so oblivious to others? For example, there's Man and his fear of weird illnesses. Every time his right knee hurts, he looks it up on Google and searches out the worst possible cause. 'Oh, my God,

I'm dying of cancer of the knee,' he tells Lady, having completed his ten seconds of research. He then goes straight to writing his will and debating which son will get the Elvis records. If only he realised the truth: neither son wants the Elvis records.

'I'm too young to die,' he weeps to Lady, once the Elvis debate has spluttered to an end. 'And this knee cancer is probably the worst cancer of them all.'

Now, I'm not a doctor – I never really bothered – but I find this diagnosis unlikely. A more probable cause of his sore-knee-itis is that he's about ten kilos overweight. More is being asked of that poor knee than can be reasonably expected. A couple of strenuous dog walks each day, and a diet in which his faithful dog was fed half his dinner each night, would lead to a medical miracle. Hallelujah! The cancer is cured! The lame can walk!

Cancer of the knee is not Man's only anxiety. He's also perpetually concerned that the house is about to be robbed. This despite THE VERY COMPETENT GUARD DOG, who is on duty, virtually 24/7, protecting the place. Apparently, my efforts are not good enough. Instead, he has this complex anti-burglary system in which, whenever the two of them go out, he sets up a battery of radios and lights and fans, before – with great significance – placing a pair of his old working boots by the front door.

'Here's the idea,' he tells Lady, every single time he does it. 'When the robber comes up, he'll think this really big bloke has just come back from work, has kicked off his boots, and is presently sitting just inside the front door, his large legs akimbo.'

Now, I'm a dog with a big vocabulary, but even I find his use of the word 'akimbo' a trifle pretentious. Lady, though, humours him. 'Great idea,' she says with no real conviction, 'I really think that will work.'

What's annoying is when they come back from their social gathering, a few hours later, he gives all the credit to that pair of old boots. 'Everything is fine, the house is safe,' says Man, before adding the self-regarding observation, 'It looks like my old boot trick worked again.'

No, mate. What worked was yours truly barking his guts out every time anyone came near the place. Your old boots had zero impact. It was your loyal dog that saved the day.

Generally, I think humans worry about the wrong things. They worry about crime when all the statistics show that crime is becoming less common. They worry about money, when all you need is a roof over your head and a good supply of chicken. And they worry about how other humans regard them, when the only view that counts is that of your own loving dog, since he or she knows you better than anyone.

Back in the bedroom, the thunderstorm has passed. That's the thing about thunderstorms, they always pass. Not so the anxieties of Man.

I emerge from under the bed to find him in a total state. By this stage, he is lying on top of the bed, whinging to Lady about – variously – his knee, the state of the planet, a problem at work, a possible resurgence of the coronavirus, and the fact that his printer has run out of ink. I can tell there is going to be a bad night ahead – sleeplessness, anxiety, bad dreams, spiking blood pressure – and so it will be a case of Clancy to the rescue.

I jump up on the bed and wait for him to start patting me. The science, after all is indisputable. As one peer-reviewed study put it: 'There is a significant decrease in both systolic and diastolic blood pressure when petting a dog with whom a companion bond has been established.'

An established 'companion bond'? That's me and Man, and sure enough, after a few minutes' more complaining, he starts patting me, while simultaneously complimenting me on my good character. His blood pressure, I can sense, is dropping by the minute. Lady gives me a pat too, as if to say, 'Thank you, Clancy, for helping him calm down.' Soon after, I hear a crash of distant thunder. I have an urge to scamper under the bed, but it sounds very distant, and besides I am quite enjoying being patted.

Here's a random thought. Maybe it's not only *human* blood pressure that responds to a session of human–dog patting. Maybe my own blood pressure goes down, even though that is not my aim. Who knows, but surely it's worthy of a scientific study: 'The Effect of Human Patting on Both Systolic and Diastolic Blood Pressure in a Dog'.

Maybe you have some ideas about how I can apply for a grant.

Hope all is well.

Love,

Clancy

Clancy always comes over as very well informed, medically speaking, but I think he just finds all this stuff on Google.

Age: **Four years and ten months**

C/- Chateau Chaos

15 June

Dear Mum and Dad,

Here's a question for you: when was the last time you saw a dog looking at themselves in the mirror? That's right. It never happens. But humans are always at it. Every morning in my city household, Man stands in front of the mirror, adjusts his hair, and then says 'Mmm, not bad.' Then Lady, who is really the better looking of the two, has a turn at the mirror, staring at her face for ages, before mumbling, 'Oh, the horror, the horror.'

It's not only them. Everywhere I go, humans seem to spend inordinate energy focusing on their appearance and that of their friends. Sometimes it's positive, sometimes negative, but it's always at the top of their minds.

'Oh, that's a lovely dress,' they'll say. Or 'Look at your great new haircut!' Or – sometimes, under their breath – 'He's a bit fat for that shirt.'

They spend a fortune buying clothes, and then go off to get an expensive dye treatment for their head fur, or – even weirder –

Archie

TJ

Pepper

Gus

Some of Clancy's friends

they pay heaps to have their body fur completely removed. Then there's the face cream, the lipstick, the aftershave, the Botox injections and the five-step microdermabrasion treatments, all followed up with the trying-on of various outfits, during which one human asks the other human, 'Do I look fat in this?' The answer to which is nearly always a downright lie.

It's all such a waste of time. Who cares about appearances? Some of my best friends look quite odd. One mate, Gus, has the body of a big dog, but with very short legs. He looks like a huge guy that's been cut off at the knees.

Do I care? No.

Does Gus care? No.

The legs maybe short, but the guy knows how to use them.

There are few animals I admire more than my friend Pepper, even though the way she does her hair is quite eccentric. It sticks up in random clumps. Some might ask, 'Exactly when were you electrocuted?' Personally, I think it's part of her charm.

Or there's Trevor, a border collie, who is entirely covered in black fur, except for one leg that's entirely white. Humans might think that Trevor looks like he's had an accident with a paint tin, but the splash of white has the advantage of making him instantly recognisable, even at a distance. I spot him immediately and go running towards him because I know he's got a fun personality.

Not all dogs, of course, look strange. I, for instance, happen to be quite handsome, with a noble jawline and large ears that can swivel in any direction. I also have two-tone fur – chocolate with a tinge of red on most of my body, with contrasting light fawn around my muzzle and chest. Somehow, it just looks 'right'. You could bring in a top fashion designer from Paris, and they'd not change a thing. '*C'est magnifique*,' is what they'd say.

But here's the point. I don't waste time thinking about it. I've never believed my appearance made me morally superior, or more intelligent, or better behaved, than a dog whose colouration is more haphazard. I understand my looks are a trick of genetics – nothing more, nothing less. When someone compliments me with the expression 'Good dog' – an occurrence which borders on the routine – they are referring to my eager and loyal character, not to the colour of my fur or the angle of my jaw.

The poet Bryon once said that dogs represented 'all the virtues of man, without his vices', and this human obsession with appearance is a case in point. There's research that says good-looking humans are assumed to be more honourable than those rated as less attractive. Other studies show that, on average, good-looking people receive higher salaries. In US elections, a taller candidate will nearly always beat a shorter one. How ridiculous is that? And then there are the children's stories told by humans –

tales in which the prince is always 'handsome', the princess is always 'beautiful', and the villain sadly blighted in the looks department.

Talk about shallow!

A dog does not judge a book by its cover. A tiny dog or a large dog, when encountered in the park, is treated with the same respect as a dog one's own size. There's no focus on the colour of another's pelt or whether the fur is worn Afro-style, clipped or shaggy. A cheaply made dog collar will never cause the new friendship to falter. A dog is a dog, except perhaps for the occasional Great Dane, which, as I've noted in one of my earlier letter's home, can create the apprehension that someone has mistakenly purchased a horse.

'Give yourself a break,' that's my message to the humans. All women are beautiful. All men are handsome. People look great in their twenties and thirties; and even better in their seventies and eighties.

We're not here for long, people. Let's enjoy it.

Anyway, that's my thought for the day.

Love,
Clancy

He's right, of course. All the same, I do wonder how Clancy became so wise when he spends so much of his time digging holes in the back lawn. Maybe he catches up on his studies in the middle of the day. What's surprising is that humans used to know this stuff. Parents would berate any child who spent too much time examining their own reflection by saying, 'It's what's inside that counts.' Or, 'All that glitters is not gold.' Or even, 'Looks are deceiving.'

I have one friend who complained about her looks in front of her mother. Rather than reassure her, the mother said, 'Since you are as plain as a pikestaff, perhaps you should learn to play the piano.' Another – this is the person who Clancy calls Lady – once said, 'Oh, Mum, what am I going to do? I'm so fat and ugly,' to which her mother replied, 'Well, you'll just have to develop a nice personality.' In other words, 'Yes, you are fat and ugly, and you haven't even developed a nice personality.' Lady, by the way, used the line in a play called Dags, which has been in production virtually ever since, so she had her own sweet revenge.

Dogs suffer none of this torment. They just accept each other. It reminds me of that Jerry Seinfeld routine about the friendships between children: 'You like cherry soda? I like cherry soda! We'll be best friends!'

And so it is with the dogs down at the park. 'You like burning around the park, doing really sharp turns? What a coincidence, because I like burning around the park, doing really sharp turns. Let's be besties.'

'You like chasing a ball? Well, I like chasing a dog who is chasing a ball. I think that means we're the perfect team.'

Of course, being accepting of others is not the only way in which dogs are superior to humans. A dog is better at smelling, that goes without saying. A dog is better at sleeping. A dog mostly has good dreams, in which his legs twitch and circle as if he's a young puppy perpetually chasing rabbits beneath an always blue sky. What bliss that must be.

Also, a dog makes the best of things. Clancy, for example, is fed at five o'clock in the afternoon, but then drinks heartily from his water bowl at precisely the moment the rest of us sit down to eat our dinner some two hours later. I'm guessing the bowl of water is not as good as a second serve of that delicious chicken he had earlier, but it joins him to the celebratory mood. He likes being part of things and knows how to engineer it.

Dogs find pleasure everywhere. Even a highly intelligent dog like Clancy can find hours of pleasure snapping his jaws at flies, though he has only once captured one and the taste was a disappointment. He enjoys it when the landline phone rings, even though, like all of us, he knows it will be a telemarketer. And he'll always respond to the doorbell, even though it's so rarely for him.

We humans sit with our problems of self-esteem, not asking for love because we secretly wonder if we deserve it. Not so the dog, secure enough in his self-belief that he'll use his wet nose to forcibly reposition a human hand so it no longer wastes time holding a book, or flicking the pages of a newspaper, or reaching for a cup of tea, but instead fulfils its proper function scratching a dog's head or rubbing a dog's tummy.

We humans are superior, perhaps, in possessing an opposable thumb — but dogs are so much better at understanding the tasks for which those dexterous human hands should always be used.

Fetching a dog's bowl, tickling a dog's ear, stroking a dog's coat.

As well as posting a dog's wise letters home.

Afterword

This book, even though it's Clancy's book, began with a story about my first dog, Darcy. Maybe it should end that way.

By the time Darcy was thirteen years old, the garden hose had been his favourite thing for at least a decade. There was always a tiny squeak when I turned on the tap, and he could hear the sound through multiple closed doors. He could sense it from suburbs away. His ears would swivel, and he would come running, insisting any intermediate doors be opened. He would stand on his hind legs in order to see out the back window. 'Oh, the hose,' he would pant. 'The hose.'

When the back door was opened, he'd shoot into the yard and stand in front of me as I watered, sometimes barking, sometimes just looking hopeful, until I sprayed him with the hose. Then he'd run around in circles, leaping and, it seemed to me, laughing, until I did it again. It was a hassle, actually. I often put off watering the garden just to save myself and the neighbours from this noisy circus. There are plants in my garden who owe their stunted growth to my Darcy-induced unwillingness to water.

Then, sometime after his fourteenth birthday, I found I could use the hose as much as I liked. Over that last year my dog became a

207

senior kelpie. His hearing went and he could no longer apprehend the squeak of the tap, even when he was there, just on the other side of the door. I felt mean as I conducted my surreptitious watering while he slept, oblivious to the fun that could be had. If only he knew the delightful aquatic activities on offer just a metre away. I felt like a married man having a secret affair under the very nose of his innocent sleeping wife. Oh, the guilt.

The lack of hearing also made him hard to find. I could no longer whistle him up when I came home at night. I would search through the garden, checking the tucked-away spots in which he liked to sleep. Then I would see the flash of his eyes in the dark as he woke up. Seeing me, he would bound out of the bushes, ears up, eyes shining, ready for anything.

This is the mystery of the older dog. He can go from snoozing pensioner to eager puppy in a second. I would watch him and think him a model for myself as I grew older. Make sure you get enough sleep, then jump up and let rip when there's something worth doing.

The lack of hearing was a problem, but in other ways he became an even better dog. He let go some of his obsessions. An example was the section of fence on our bush block. Fourteen years before, when Darcy was still a puppy, I threw a dead sheep carcass over that fence to stop him from eating it. He spent the day staring through the fence, patrolling up and down. It became a habit, an *idée fixe*, until every time we visited he would bound from the car to run up and down alongside that section of fence, eventually wearing down a little slot in the earth. We would call him away, of course, but he would always slink back to his task, miserable and footsore, answering to an inner compulsion, the origin of which he'd long forgotten.

As an older dog, he would still tumble from the car when we arrived and attend to his habitual duty. But after half an hour he would stop as if to say, 'Really I've done enough; get someone else in to do the job. Me? I'm going easy on myself. I'm retired.'

Again a life lesson: as you grow older, it may be sensible to give up the obsessions that made your life miserable, especially when you can no longer recall why they became so compelling in the first place.

Darcy's antipathies also began to wane as he aged; the figures in life who had brought anxiety or fear seemed to lose their power. He no longer freaked out when I handled the Wheelie Bin. For fourteen years he had imagined the thing was evil and about to overpower me. For fourteen years he had barked his urgent warning, 'Beware! Beware!' Then, late in life, he appeared to accept the reality: while the Wheelie Bin sometimes resists, it is always defeated during the weekly battle in which I wrestle it down the driveway and onto the nature strip.

The evidence is in. I have its measure.

Darcy's more positive passions, though, remained undiminished to the last. In his case, the passion for cheese – shared with Clancy – the possibility of its appearance tracked minute by minute, with careful viewing of anyone who arose from the couch and might be heading towards the fridge. Who knows, but they might return with cheese? As Darcy's handsome head lifted and followed our movements, I noted another life lesson: there's nothing wrong with an appreciation of the finer things.

Guilty over my surreptitious watering, I remember feeding him a fragment of cheese and tickling those once-acute ears. He had given me so many lessons and here was another: as we grow older we should let our passions be maintained, while the negative stuff fades away.

I decided, next time, to make sure he could see me when the watering began.

After Darcy died, I wrote about him in the newspaper, and how hard it was to deal with the death of a dog. At one point, I said how weird it felt that my dog's death created feelings in me stronger than the loss of some human friends. The thought made me uncomfortable, but it was the truth. In the weeks afterwards, I was overwhelmed by emails and letters, many with stories so vivid and compelling they have stayed with me for years.

In so many, the dog played the role of lifesaver.

One of the first letters I received was written by a former soldier, a veteran of Australia's deployment to the Middle East, now diagnosed with post-traumatic stress disorder. With courageous honesty, he described himself as 'a very solitary man with no friends anymore'. His supportive and loving wife suggested a dog could help, so they visited the pound and found a puppy. In his letter, he described his meeting with his new friend: 'He climbed me like a monkey climbs a tree and licked my face. I knew I had found a partner, a bit of a rascal and keen to show affection, a bit like me.'

He described the bond the two of them formed over the six years that followed. 'I know that, if asked, he would follow me into battle … he has shown me there is joy in our bizarre mixed-up world and helped me see through the fog of manipulation and carnage that is war. He looks at me in a way that is so honest, so true that only my wife can emulate … I reckon he has taught me more about myself than I ever could have learned alone.'

The letter was full of love and gratitude, and of how this tiny dog was helping a soldier slowly heal the wounds of war.

Then there was a letter from a dog owner in a rural town, describing the scene after an arsonist had set off a blaze. 'I was trapped by the flames and was screaming to the fire brigade for help. But who came bursting through the wall of flames? My dog leapt up onto my chest and looked me in the eye as if to say "we die together, dad".'

The two were finally rescued, by which time the dog was so badly burned he was given little hope of survival. Within a few weeks he had recovered and was 'bouncing around like a pup', but the legacy of that rush into the flames was blindness for the dog's last two years of life.

His owner wrote admiringly: 'Providing we didn't move anything in the house or garden, he could navigate his way around with total ease. He even invented new games that he could play due to his blindness.'

More notes from dog owners came each day in the weeks after Darcy's death. I struggled to answer them, my tears coming afresh as people wrote about animals both alive and long departed. One email came from a farmer, way out in the Far West of New South Wales. He expressed his condolences for the loss of Darcy and then told his own story.

'My dog saved my life in 2005 when I was about to commit suicide. I had gotten close the previous two nights and this time I was just sitting there in some kind of existential daze. Suddenly, my dog (a black dog!) got out of his bed and shoved his head into my lap, ears down, a slight whimper and his tail wagging slowly. I'll never forget the look in his eyes.'

He added, 'He stayed very close to me over the next few weeks as I was getting treated. The dogs seem to know more about us than what we do.'

I've removed the names of the dogs in these letters to preserve people's privacy, although there's something touching about the playful, scrappy names carried by these heroic animals. The dogs featured in those stories all have names along the lines of Fang or Fluff or Fudge, Ro-Ro, Razzer or Ruff, but that doesn't stop them behaving as if they were shining knights from an Arthurian legend.

Others wrote about how the memory never fades, and posted black-and-white photos of dogs from childhood, telling stories still vividly remembered. Some said they'd refused to replace a scratched door, or kept some chewed toys, as a nod to memory. And so many talked – like me, with a mixture of guilt, surprise and wonder – about the way they had cried more freely, with less restraint, about the loss of their dog than they had over a lost parent or friend. 'I was more broken when the dog died than when my dad died,' said one.

If I were a scholar of linguistics, I could whip up a statistical analysis of the words most frequently used in the hundreds of letters and emails I received. 'Lucky' was probably the word most often used, as in 'How lucky are we to have them in our lives?'

'Privilege' was also common, as in 'It was a privilege to know her,' and, of course, 'loyal' appears again and again.

And, when describing any dog, there is the inevitable appreciation of beauty: 'so handsome', 'so pretty', 'so good looking'.

In the piece about Darcy's death, I called him the 'best dog that ever was', and I stick to that claim. But – here's an interesting thing – it emerges that nearly everyone else happens to have 'the best dog that ever was'.

It's an assessment, I'm convinced, that's true in every case.

Especially when it comes to Clancy.

It's not a competition...

Acknowledgements

From Clancy

I'd like to acknowledge support and inspiration from all my friends at the dog park – Pepper (an associate of Lady and Lady), Archie, Watto, Lucky, Dougal, Gus, Georgie and the rest. Full marks, also, to Man and Lady, who always seem to keep the tucker up.

From Richard

Thanks to Judy Herskovits and Lizzie Elliott, to Joan Carden (who keeps Clancy supplied with daily treats in the park); to Lola's pals Connie and Jim Salmon; and to all the other fun people in our local dog park, especially Nick who keeps my skin beautiful. I love that Clancy introduced me to you all. Thanks, as always, to the fabulous people at HarperCollins, in particular Mary Rennie and Brigitta Doyle, as well as to Jeanne Ryckmans and Anthony Blair at Cameron's Management. And, at the *Sydney Morning Herald*, I'd like to thank my dog-loving editors Shona Martyn, Helen Pitt and Melanie Kembrey, as well as Melanie's dog Bear, who always demanded 'more Clancy!'

The quotes sending up dogs, as cited by Clancy, came from Dave Barry in his 1988 column for the *Miami Herald*; from Merrill Markoe in her 1992 book *What the Dogs Have Taught Me*; and from George Carlin in a stand-up show from Carnegie Hall in 1983. Whatever Clancy thinks, I know all of them – especially Merrill Markoe – to be dog lovers. I also note, without judgement, that one of Clancy's lines – 'I'm not a doctor – I never really bothered' – appears to be stolen from 'The Blood Donor' episode of the BBC comedy series *Hancock*, featuring Tony Hancock, first transmitted on 23 June 1961 and written by Ray Galton and Alan Simpson. How he has access to these things, I just don't know.

Thanks, finally, to Daniel Mendelsohn for kindly allowing me to quote from his translation of *The Odyssey*; to photographer Jon Lewis for his perfect shot of a young Clancy; and to Cathy Wilcox, who has proved yet again that she is the world's best cartoonist. And, as always, to Lady, aka Debra Oswald.